THE ACTS

An Exposition

by
CHARLES R. ERDMAN

PREFACE BY EARL F. ZEIGLER

THE WESTMINSTER PRESS

PHILADELPHIA

Published by The Westminster Press ®
Philadelphia, Pennsylvania

PRINTED IN THE UNITED STATES OF AMERICA

PREFACE

In the eighth chapter of The Acts, Dr. Luke relates the experience of Philip the "deacon" who was providentially sent to intercept the chariot of a traveler on the Gaza Road. The chariot was occupied by an educated and God-fearing high official in the court of the queen of the Ethiopians. The man had made the long trip from Ethiopia to Jersualem to worship, to learn more about the Jewish faith, and to participate in one of the feasts. He was probably what the Jews called a "God-fearer," a Gentile who had been attracted by the Jewish idea of one supreme God, and by the higher moral tone of Judaism.

While in Jerusalem he had perhaps purchased one or two scrolls of Scripture. Now on his way home as he rode he was reading aloud from the scroll of Isaiah, but he was perplexed about the meaning of a certain passage. At this psychological moment Philip politely called to him, "Do you understand what you are reading?" "How can I, unless some one guides me?" came the plaintive rejoinder. Philip instantly accepted an invitation to enter the chariot, and as the horses plodded along the two men communed on the Word. *Philip became the expositor.* "Beginning with this scripture [from Isaiah] he told him the good news of Jesus." Now that the official of the queen "understood" he requested baptism. Philip welcomed this man of high spiritual potential into the church. The court of the queen soon had the witness of a man in Christ.

The reader of this preface does not need to be told that the foregoing illustration is a relevant example of the value of an expositor to aid the student in a more complete understanding of Scripture. Even expositors consult and learn from other expositors. Mind must meet mind and spirit commune with spirit to bring forth the rich treasures of the Bible. And is not this one of the ways in which the Holy Spirit works—the Holy Spirit who is to bring all things to our remembrance?

This volume on The Acts is one of seventeen similar books in each of which Dr. Charles R. Erdman is the expositor. His name assures the reader of scholarship, simplicity of style, deep insights, practicality, awareness of student needs, and above all, a genuine dedication to further the gospel of Jesus Christ, the only-begotten Son of God.

Dr. Erdman is acquainted with the views of other expositors, and if he cannot agree fully with some of them, his irenic spirit never questions the integrity of their research. Dr. Erdman does let his readers know what he believes and why, and he also allows for variant opinions. His outline of the text of The Acts provides a ready guide to the student. His exposition, section by section, brings to the surface many ideas and insights for pastors, teachers in the church school, students in college and seminary, but even more important, guidance in spiritual living for the young person or the man or woman who looks to the Bible for daily spiritual food.

This paperback edition has been printed from completely new type and plates. Numerous printings of former editions had worn the old plates too badly to be of further use.

The one thing that has not worn out is The Acts itself as written by Dr. Luke. Whoever would know the exciting account of the origin and growth of the early church will find it in no other writing. But the Christian church is facing another new era. We Christians must know The Acts to receive Spirit guidance in our witnessing to the faith.

EARL F. ZEIGLER

FOREWORD

In peace or war, in the past or present, no project has been so bold, no adventure so thrilling, as the enterprise of carrying the gospel to the whole world. The Acts tells how this work was begun, and how the good news was brought across the imperial provinces from Jerusalem to Rome, not by a single messenger or by individual effort, but by the rapid extension of the Christian church. The book is a record of heroic achievement and inspired eloquence, a treasury of truths vital to believers, a manual of methods for evangelists and missionaries, and a witness to the unceasing activity of the living Christ and to the present power of his divine Spirit. Those to whom the story is quite familiar will be the most eager to read it anew, for they know best its value and its charm.

INTRODUCTION

THE AUTHOR

It was a high honor to compose the most significant chapters in the history of the Christian church; yet the author of The Acts, who alone relates the origin of the most significant society and of the mightiest movement in the world, makes no mention of his own name. There is little doubt, however, that this author was "Luke, the beloved physician," the faithful friend and companion of Paul. This belief is supported: (1) by a constant tradition extending back to the earliest centuries; (2) by the fact that the same writer composed the Third Gospel, which fact appears in the dedication of both books to Theophilus, in the similarity of style and spirit, in the identity of language, more than forty words being found in both books which appear nowhere else in the New Testament, in the common use of technical medical terms, in the opening reference of The Acts to a "former treatise" which was a life of Christ; therefore, as the Gospel always has been assigned to Luke, it is evident that he also must have written The Acts; (3) by the fact that in certain sections of the book the author writes in the first person, using the pronouns "we" and "us," thus modestly intimating that at the time of the events described he was associated with Paul; and when the circumstances recorded are compared with references made to Luke, by name, in the Epistles, it becomes evident that of all the associates of Paul only Luke could have written these passages. That these passages came from the same pen as the rest of the book is evident from the unity of plan and style and vocabulary.

It appears, then, that the author was a Greek by birth, possibly a native of Antioch, a man of culture and refinement, an extensive traveler, modest, intelligent, sympathetic, loyal. He accompanied Paul from Troas to Philippi on that memorable journey when the great apostle brought the gospel tidings from Asia to Europe; on a subsequent journey he returned with Paul from Philippi to Jerusalem; he was with him during his imprisonment at Caesarea, he journeyed with him to Rome, and there in the dreary days of confinement, he showed the unique fidelity which Paul records in that memorable phrase: "Only Luke is with me."

Surely this writer was well equipped for his immortal task. For his earlier narratives he had opportunity to secure materials from Mark at Rome, from Philip at Caesarea, from Paul and his companions on their long journeys and during the repeated periods in prison; but the most brilliant passages are those which he writes as an eyewitness, when he again lives through the stirring scenes which by his genius have become unfading, inspiring pictures for the Christian world.

The Aim

Luke shows himself a historian, not of the third or second but of the very first rank, by his absolute accuracy, by the definiteness of his aim, and by the consequent careful selection and consistent use of his literary material. He had in mind one clear purpose; to that every narrative is related, by that all needless details are excluded, with that before him he gave to his work unity, clearness, force; as a result, we have here no mere disconnected memoirs, no chance extracts from a diary, no careless collection of apostolic traditions, but a finished treatise, a monument of artistic skill. His definite aim was to write a history of the formation and early growth of the church; or, in the words of a modern scholar, it was to compose "a special history of the planting and extension of the Church by the . . . establishment of radiating centers at certain salient points throughout a large part of the Roman Em-

pire, beginning at Jerusalem and ending at Rome." Thus
it was not the purpose of the writer to produce biographies
of Peter or Paul or other apostles; he described these characters only insofar as their activities were concerned with
his main purpose of showing how the church was formed,
how broadened to receive Gentiles, how extended from
Jerusalem to Rome. So, too, it was evidently not his aim
to write all that he knew of the history of any local church,
at Jerusalem or Antioch or Philippi, but only to show how
the witnessing of Christian messengers resulted in the establishment of such societies, and how they aided in the
work of proclaiming the gospel to the whole world.

The Theme

There is thus one great theme to which every paragraph
of the narrative is related, namely, "The Church Witnessing for Christ." It should be noted, then, that the writer
is continually concerned with a history of the church. He
is not describing the growth of local organizations, but he
has in mind a new and a unique body in which Jews and
Gentiles were united on a perfect equality. Such a union
had been intimated by Christ (John 10:16), but "the
mystery" of such a "body" was not fully revealed until
after his resurrection (Eph. 3:6). The Acts shows how
this body came into being, how it gradually developed
from a local sect into a universal brotherhood, how by it
Christianity was emancipated from Judaism and became
a world religion. Luke traced its extension throughout
the Empire as far as the city of Rome; he shows that it em-
braced representatives of many nationalities and was established in many provinces, but was always one united
body. In later days of denominational divisions and of
sectarian strife there is something refreshing, inspiring, if
not rebuking, in this picture of the apostolic church.

It should be noted, further, that this church was a witnessing body. The Acts is not so much concerned with the

development of Christian life or the application of Christian truth as with the work of preaching the gospel. Thus it may be well to follow the popular custom and to suggest, as a key verse, the eighth verse of the first chapter: "Ye shall receive power, when the Holy Spirit is come upon you: and ye shall be my witnesses both in Jerusalem, and in all Judæa and Samaria, and unto the uttermost part of the earth." The witnessing was to be done by the power of the Holy Spirit. In no book of the Bible can more be learned as to the Spirit's divine office than in The Acts, in none are there more marvelous records of his might; so that by some writers the narrative has been called "The Acts of the Holy Spirit."

How this witnessing was done in Jerusalem is related in the first seven chapters of the book; the witnessing in Judea and Samaria is recorded in chapters eight to twelve; and the remainder of the narrative concerns the witnessing "unto the uttermost part of the earth." As to the nature of this witnessing, the most casual reading of the story shows that it was no mere heralding of the truth, regardless of results; but it was undertaken with care and method, and was so directed as to secure the establishment of churches which became permanent centers of enlarging effort.

Again, it should be noted that this witnessing was for Christ. Nor does this mean merely that he was the Person to whom witness was borne. It is true that the substance of the witness was invariably the death, the resurrection, the present power, and the coming Kingdom of Christ; but when Christ declared that the disciples were to be his witnesses, he meant that they were to be his instruments, his mouthpieces; he was to do the witnessing through them. In the first verse of the story, Luke has referred to his Gospel as written "concerning all that Jesus began both to do and to teach, until the day in which he was received up"; and he has been thought to imply that this second "treatise" would concern what Jesus continued to do. It is a question whether the word "began" was so intended by the writer; but the fact remains that such is indeed the character of the book; The Acts does record the continuing activity of Christ; he is the mighty Worker in all the stirring scenes of the story, his message is being spoken, his power is being manifested, his will is being done.

Some, unwisely, have pressed even farther the word "began," to make it indicate that, as the Gospel contained great fundamental words and works of Christ's earthly ministry, so in The Acts the writer recorded only certain, selected, initial deeds and teachings of our risen Lord. While this forces too far the single word, it does call to mind the truth that this is a book of beginnings. The author has shown how the work was commenced and how foundations were laid at certain important centers; he has described the origins of societies and activities, and has then passed on to other incidents and scenes. His is a narrative of how the church began its universal witnessing for Christ.

The Title

It accords well with this evident selection of material that the book, in the earliest existing manuscript, is designated "Acts," and thus the American Revised Version gives as its title "The Acts," by which is meant a narrative of certain notable deeds. As other books, however, were being published under such titles as "Acts of Peter and Paul," "Acts of Timothy," and so forth, it became necessary to define more exactly the original "treatise" of "The Acts." Thus in various manuscripts such titles as "Acts of the Apostles," "Acts of the Holy Apostles," or "The Acts of the Apostles" are found. The last is possibly the most familiar title and is said to be as old as the second century. While it is not wholly objectionable, as indicating important achievements of the apostles, the difficulty is evident, in that other men than apostles have a prominent place in the narrative, and to most of the apostles no part is assigned. The more modern title, "Acts of Apostles," is preferred by many, as it accurately, but indefinitely, indicates some acts of certain apostles.

THE OUTLINE

Two apostles, Peter and Paul, are especially prominent in the narrative, and the account of their activities has suggested a popular division of the book into two parts: (1) The evangelization of the Jews, by Peter, the apostle of the circumcision. (Chs. 1 to 12.) (2) The evangelization of the Gentiles, by Paul, the apostle to the Gentiles. (Chs. 13 to 28.) It may be well, however, to subdivide the first part, and to follow the analysis suggested in connection with the Great Commission in Acts 1:8: (1) The witness in Jerusalem. (Chs. 1:1 to 8:3.) (2) The witness in Judea and Samaria. (Chs. 8:4 to 12:25.) (3) The witness "unto the uttermost part of the earth." (Chs. 13 to 28.) The advantage of the latter division is the opportunity of noting the transitional character of the narrative in chs. 8 to 12, where the church is widening its horizon and is receiving into its membership others than Jews, and so is being prepared for its universal mission. Thus we can trace in each division a development in the character of the church, and the sections may be defined as follows: (1) The founding of the church and its great initial experiences. (2) The broadening of the church from a Jewish sect to a universal brotherhood. (3) The extension of the church, as a body of witnesses, bearing its testimony to the whole world. The narrative, however, must not be dissected too coldly. It forms a unity; it throbs with life; it thrills with emotion; it stirs the reader to venture forth and share the heroic enterprise the first scenes of which are here depicted, the matchless endeavor to witness for Christ in all the world.

THE OUTLINE

I
THE FOUNDING OF THE CHURCH

II
THE BROADENING OF THE CHURCH

III
THE EXTENSION OF THE CHURCH

I

THE FOUNDING
OF THE CHURCH

THE WITNESS IN JERUSALEM
Chs. 1:1 to 8:3

A. INTRODUCTORY Ch. 1

1. THE ASCENSION OF CHRIST   Ch. 1:1-11

*1 The former treatise I made, O Theophilus, concerning
all that Jesus began both to do and to teach, 2 until the day
in which he was received up, after that he had given commandment through the Holy Spirit unto the apostles whom
he had chosen: 3 to whom he also showed himself alive
after his passion by many proofs, appearing unto them by
the space of forty days, and speaking the things concerning
the kingdom of God: 4 and, being assembled together
with them, he charged them not to depart from Jerusalem,
but to wait for the promise of the Father, which,* said *he,
ye heard from me: 5 for John indeed baptized with water;
but ye shall be baptized in the Holy Spirit not many days
hence.*

*6 They therefore, when they were come together, asked
him, saying, Lord, dost thou at this time restore the kingdom to Israel? 7 And he said unto them, It is not for you
to know times or seasons, which the Father hath set within
his own authority. 8 But ye shall receive power, when the
Holy Spirit is come upon you: and ye shall be my witnesses
both in Jerusalem, and in all Judæa and Samaria, and unto
the uttermost part of the earth. 9 And when he had said
these things, as they were looking, he was taken up; and a
cloud received him out of their sight. 10 And while they
were looking stedfastly into heaven as he went, behold two*

men stood by them in white apparel; 11 who also said,
Ye men of Galilee, why stand ye looking into heaven? this
Jesus, who was received up from you into heaven, shall so
come in like manner as ye beheld him going into heaven.

The book could not open more fittingly than with this
story thus told, for the author is to write of the church and
its witness for Christ, and this story at once fixes the
thought upon the living, divine Lord, the Head of the
church, who by his Spirit is to unite his followers into one
body, who is to empower this body for service and is to
direct it in all its work of testifying for him. Then, too,
the story is so told as to present the substance of the witness, for within its brief compass mention is made of the
works and words of Christ, of his "passion," of his resurrection, of his ascension, of the gift of his Spirit, of his second coming and his Kingdom; and as we review The Acts
we find that these are the very truths to which testimony
is being borne continually by the witnessing church.
These are the themes which the church ever emphasizes,
when she is faithfully witnessing for her Lord.

Thus it is evident that the opening paragraph (vs.
1-11), like the rest of the first chapter (vs. 12-26), is introductory to the main action of the book; its most important statements concern the ascension (vs. 2, 9, 11); but it
also contains the author's preface (vs. 1-5), the Great
Commission (vs. 6-8), and the promise of Christ's return
(vs. 10-11).

a. When compared with the introduction to the Third
Gospel (Luke 1:1-4), the preface to The Acts (ch.
1:1-5) is less formal and from a literary point of view less
perfect; yet in relation to the narrative which follows, it is
more significant, for it declares that the Person whose
words and works are recorded in "the former treatise" is
he of whom Luke is again to write, and it affirms that this
Jesus is risen from the dead and ascended into heaven; and
it intimates that "the acts" which this book records are

wrought by his Spirit through the agency of his apostles.

In each instance Luke addresses his work to Theophilus (beloved of God), of whom nothing further is known, although he is supposed to have been a distinguished Gentile convert to Christianity residing in Rome. Luke here summarizes his Gospel by calling it a "treatise . . . concerning all that Jesus began both to do and to teach, until the day in which he was received up." Thus the ascension, which was the culminating feature of the Gospel narrative is the starting point for The Acts. Luke here reminds Theophilus that previous to his ascension Jesus "had given commandment through the Holy Spirit unto the apostles," and that this commandment concerned the preaching of Christ to "all the nations"; The Acts is now to relate how this preaching was begun in Jerusalem and continued as far as the imperial city of Rome. In his reference to the resurrection, Luke adds to the records of his Gospel the statements that the appearances of Jesus, who "showed himself alive after his passion," were numerous and convincing and were continued at intervals during "the space of forty days." This resurrection is to be the supreme message of the apostles in the scenes which follow; it is the best attested fact in history; it is the cornerstone of the Christian faith. The teaching of Christ, during the days between his resurrection and his ascension, was "concerning the kingdom of God," which in all its perfection is to be established upon earth. There first must be, however, a universal proclamation of the Gospel; and therefore in the crowning statement of his "preface" Luke repeats the promise of the baptism of the Spirit, by whose power the preaching, which The Acts records, is to be done. This promise Jesus called "the promise of the Father," because God had given it through inspired prophets, including John the Baptist, but it was also the promise of Jesus himself, frequently made to his disciples, particularly on the night before his crucifixion, and again, as recorded by Luke, after his resurrection. This promise was of a baptism strikingly contrasted with that of John; the latter was momentary, in the physical element of water, implying a cleansing from sin; the former was to consist in an abiding relation to a Person whose continual presence was to transform character and to impart power for service. For the fulfillment of this promise the disciples were to wait in Jerusalem, and when it was fulfilled the followers of Christ would be equipped for the work which The Acts relates. Such, in brief, is "the preface" to the book; it brings an important message, that all witness for Christ not only must declare his works and words but must present him as the risen and ascended Lord, and that such witness can be given only by those who are baptized in his Holy Spirit.

b. The Great Commission (vs. 6-8) is given with a somewhat altered accent at the close of each of the four Gospels. The substance is ever the same, but Matthew (ch. 28:18) sounds the note of kingly "authority"; Mark (ch. 16:15-18) emphasizes the accompanying divine power; Luke (ch. 24:46-49) makes prominent the universal witness; John (ch. 20:21-22) lays stress upon the spiritual issue of the work. Of course, all elements are, in a measure, common to these reports of the one final command; and it is interesting to note how, in The Acts, all are emphatically combined. Here the "commission" is given in connection with a question asked by the disciples of their risen Lord: "Dost thou at this time restore the kingdom to Israel?" Jesus does not correct any misconceptions in reference to the Kingdom which may have lingered in their minds. Their belief was essentially true. Jesus encourages them to expect that there would be a restitution; how much larger and more wonderful and more spiritual than they dreamed, he does not pause to explain. They had the right conception. Peter in his "second sermon" (Acts 3:21) calls it the "restoration of all things." True blessedness for Israel and for the world was sure to come; but there were certain events to precede, certain conditions to be fulfilled; chief among which, on the human side, was the universal preaching of the gospel. Just when this would be accomplished and the perfected Kingdom of God would appear, it was not given to the disciples to know; exact dates and epochs, "times or seasons . . . the Father hath set within his own authority." The disciples must first accomplish their task, and for this work they would be equipped when they should be filled with the Holy Spirit. This power came upon them mightily at Pentecost, and it ever since has been residing upon those who are completely surrendered to do the will of their Lord. The immediate task, then, of the disciples, and now of all who truly pray, "Thy kingdom come," is that of witnessing for Christ. "Ye shall be my witnesses," however, does not mean merely that Christ is the object or subject of the testimony, but that the witnesses belong to him, and that through them the living Lord is prosecuting the work by the power of his divine Spirit.

The sphere of this witnessing was to be universal. "In Jerusalem [city evangelization], and in all Judæa and Samaria [home missions], and unto the uttermost part of the earth [foreign missions]" was the command. Just how it was carried out is the story of The Acts.

c. The ascension of Christ (v. 9) includes two great realities: (1) he then passed from the sphere of the seen and temporal into the sphere of the unseen and eternal; and (2) he then assumed "all authority . . . in heaven and on earth." The event is quite distinct from the resurrection which took place forty days before, and also from "the gift of the Holy Spirit" which occurred ten days later, at Pentecost. In the preaching of the apostles and in their inspired writings this event held a prominent place. It is possible that it should be given more serious consideration and a new emphasis in the present day.

(1) Ever since his resurrection Jesus had been meeting frequently with his disciples, eating and drinking with them, teaching them and "speaking the things concerning the kingdom of God"; now he formally and finally with-

draws from them: "a cloud received him out of their sight"; henceforth he will be an unseen Presence, he will speak to them by his Spirit. "He was taken up"; but we are not to suppose that he passed through infinite spaces, and is now at a vast distance, in some remote sphere. There is no "up" or "down" in this universe. To say that he "ascended" is a correct but merely conventional use of speech; it fitly describes his disappearance from earthly sight and from material conditions into the heavenly and spiritual.

It was at this time, and not at his resurrection, that our Lord assumed "the body of his glory." His resurrection was literal and real; the very same body which was laid in the tomb came forth from the tomb; in it were the nail prints and the mark of the spear; it was a body which could partake of food, which was made of "flesh and bones" (Luke 24:39, 42). Christ's leaving the tomb, his appearing behind closed doors in the upper room, his disappearing suddenly at Emmaus, were miracles no more remarkable than his walking upon the sea, and were performed in the same body. When he ascended, however, the body of our Lord was transformed, was glorified; "flesh and blood cannot inherit the kingdom of God," and the body in which Christ appeared in "the upper room" with his disciples, differed in essence from that in which he now is, "seated on the right hand of God." Such a bodily transformation as Christ experienced at his ascension was a fitting termination to his earthly ministry. As his birth had been miraculous, so, too, was his withdrawal into the region and order of the unseen; and the incarnation and the ascension well may be associated in thought. This transformation is an example and an assurance of the change which will be experienced by believers when Christ returns; they will "be changed" from mortal to immortal, and caught up "to meet the Lord in the air" (I Cor. 15:51-53; I Thess. 4:13-18). This transformation is further used as a symbol of the present spiritual experience of those who, by faith, are not only raised from death but are now seated in "heavenly places, in Christ."

(2) Even more important is the fact that, at the time of his ascension, Jesus assumed universal power. He can no longer be regarded as a mere human teacher, a prophet, a martyr; he now enters the glory which he had with the Father "before the world was"; he again exists "in the form of God"; as the Creed states: "He ascended into heaven, and sitteth on the right hand of God the Father Almighty"; as he declares in the Apocalypse, "I also overcame, and sat down with my Father in his throne." Such a conception of what is meant by an ascended Christ inspires every reader with new hope and confidence; and such a picture forms a fitting introduction to The Acts, for it fixes the thought upon Christ, the Head of the church, occupying the place of supreme power in the universe, and so able to guide, control, and protect his witnesses in their work of worldwide testimony.

d. The disciples were encouraged to undertake their task, not only by the assurance of the ultimate establishment of the Kingdom and by the expected gift of the Holy Spirit but also by the promise of Christ's return (vs. 10-11). This came to them as they stood "looking stedfastly into heaven," wondering and distressed at the departure of their Lord. It came by the lips of the angels, "two men . . . in white apparel"; fitting messengers these were, for angels had heralded the birth of Christ, and angels announced his resurrection; how natural that they should predict his return! They prefaced their promise by a question: "Ye men of Galilee, why stand ye looking into heaven?" No time was to be lost in mourning and regret; it was true their Lord had vanished from their sight, but someday he would reappear; meanwhile there was a work for them to do and in its faithful accomplishment they were to be inspired ever by this blessed hope: "This Jesus, who was received up from you into heaven, shall so come in like manner as ye beheld him going into heaven." Personal, visible, bodily, local, this coming is to be. The angels did not refer to the gift at Pentecost, which was the manifestation of a spiritual Presence, nor to the destruction of Jerusalem or other events now past, much less to the death of believers; they spoke of the future return of Christ, when the triumph of his cause will be made complete and an age of glory and righteousness will begin. No wonder the disciples were comforted and, as Luke (ch. 24:52) tells us, "returned to Jerusalem with great joy." No promise is more full of divine cheer; none has proved to be a greater stimulus to evangelistic and missionary enterprise. The Acts tells us how the disciples went forth to preach the gospel in all the world, expecting and looking for their Lord to return and to establish finally his Kingdom.

2. THE DISCIPLES IN JERUSALEM   Ch. 1:12-26

This section, like the opening verses of the chapter, may be regarded, not improperly, as introductory to the main narrative of The Acts. The great theme of the book is "The Church Witnessing for Christ," and here attention is fixed upon the disciples in Jerusalem, the elements of the church, its first members, and the official witnesses, those specially authorized to testify to the resurrection of Christ.

(a) Waiting for the Promise   Ch. 1:12-14

12 Then returned they unto Jerusalem from the mount called Olivet, which is nigh unto Jerusalem, a sabbath day's journey off. 13 And when they were come in, they went up into the upper chamber, where they were abiding; both Peter and John and James and Andrew, Philip and Thomas, Bartholomew and Matthew, James the son of Alphæus, and Simon the Zealot, and Judas the son of James. 14 These all with one accord continued stedfastly in prayer, with the women, and Mary the mother of Jesus, and with his brethren.

The picture of the disciples waiting for the fulfillment of the "promise" is full of interest. After beholding the ascension of Christ, the eleven disciples returned to Jerusalem from the Mount of Olives, "which is nigh unto Jerusalem, a sabbath day's journey off," that is, not more than a thousand paces, not farther than a pious Jew would walk upon a Sabbath. Thus the ascension was virtually from Jerusalem, from within the sacred precincts, and the Holy City was to be the scene of the first witnessing for Christ, as it had been of his most significant ministry, of his death and resurrection and ascension. It is notable that the disciples returned to Jerusalem. This was due wholly to the command of their Lord, "not to depart from Jerusalem, but to wait for the promise of the Father." Naturally they would have fled from the city; it was for them a place of peril, and their homes were in Galilee; but there was a divine purpose in having the witness begin at Jerusalem; it may have been a place of danger, but it was the place of widest possible influence. So as servants of Christ "we have all to ask, not where we shall be most at ease, but where we shall be most efficient as witnesses for Christ, and to remember that very often the presence of adversaries makes the door 'great and effectual.' "

The exact room "where they were abiding," that is, where they met from day to day, is not known; it is called "the upper chamber" and was quite probably the scene of the Last Supper, the very place where Christ had appeared to the ten disciples on the evening after his resurrection, and a week later to the same company and Thomas.

In noting the names of "the eleven," it is to be remembered that Judas is dead. In comparison with the lists given by Matthew (ch. 10:2-4) and Mark (ch. 3:16-19) it will be found that they are divided into the same three groups: "Peter and John and James and Andrew, Philip and Thomas and Bartholomew and Matthew, James the son of Alphæus, and Simon the Zealot, and Judas the son of James." The last named was called Thaddeus in the

Gospels; and Bartholomew is to be identified with Nathanael, the "Israelite" in whom Jesus saw "no guile." Of all those enumerated here only three are mentioned in this book so commonly called "The Acts of the Apostles," yet we need have no doubt that they all bore notable testimony for Christ even though the sphere of their activities lay aside from the immediate purpose of the historian.

In addition to "the eleven" Luke tells us that in the sacred circle in the upper room there were present certain women, probably those who had aided Jesus in the days of his public ministry (Luke 8:1-3; 23:55); also, "Mary the mother of Jesus," whose name does not appear again in the New Testament; and lastly the "brethren" of Jesus, who before his resurrection had not believed in him, but one of whom soon rises to the place of supreme leadership in the church in Jerusalem. Taking them all in all, the persons who composed this group were of humble station, of modest means, and of moderate ability, yet united and empowered by the Spirit of Christ, they formed the most important society and achieved the most notable work in the history of the world.

They met in that upper room for prayer; and in such gatherings the most significant Christian movements ever have been begun. They were asking for the fulfillment of a promise; this always gives assurance in prayer. The Lord had promised them a new and mighty manifestation of his Spirit; that it was to come at Pentecost we know, and we now see the symbolic fitness of the day, and the opportunity it would give for witnessing to the crowds which would then throng the sacred city; but the disciples in the upper room did not know the time appointed or the reasons for the delay; still, "these all with one accord continued stedfastly in prayer"; and The Acts records the result, and strengthens every group of believers to persevere in united intercession, trusting that the answer will be more blessed and abiding than the most confident dare ask or think.

b. Electing an Apostle   Ch. 1:15-26

15 And in these days Peter stood up in the midst of the brethren, and said (and there was a multitude of persons gathered together, about a hundred and twenty), 16 Brethren, it was needful that the scripture should be fulfilled, which the Holy Spirit spake before by the mouth of David concerning Judas, who was guide to them that took Jesus. 17 For he was numbered among us, and received his portion in this ministry. 18 (Now this man obtained a field with the reward of his iniquity; and falling headlong, he burst asunder in the midst, and all his bowels gushed out. 19 And it became known to all the dwellers at Jerusalem; insomuch that in their language that field was called Akeldama, that is, The field of blood.) 20 For it is written in the books of Psalms,

Let his habitation be made desolate,
And let no man dwell therein:
and,
His office let another take.
21 Of the men therefore that have companied with us all the time that the Lord Jesus went in and went out among us, 22 beginning from the baptism of John, unto the day that he was received up from us, of these must one become a witness with us of his resurrection. 23 And they put forward two, Joseph called Barsabbas, who was surnamed Justus, and Matthias. 24 And they prayed, and said, Thou, Lord, who knowest the hearts of all men, show of these two the one whom thou hast chosen, 25 to take the place in this ministry and apostleship from which Judas fell away, that he might go to his own place. 26 And they gave lots of them; and the lot fell upon Matthias; and he was numbered with the eleven apostles.

In recent years there has been an increasing custom of censuring the early Christians for their action in electing an apostle to fill the place made vacant by Judas. It seems to require, however, considerable temerity to criticize men who, for forty days, had been receiving instruction from the risen Christ, and who, since his ascension, had been passing the hours in united prayer. Then, too, the action was taken, not by the apostles alone, but by the whole company of Christians, and with no dissenting voice. Most significant of all, Luke, the inspired historian, finds no fault with the procedure. The criticism arises wholly from the imagination of modern readers. It is based upon the fact that in The Acts no further mention is made of the apostle who was chosen; but it is quite as true that, henceforth, with very few exceptions, all the apostles are passed by in silence, and never again are named. The criticism is made in the supposed interest of Paul, who, it is claimed, was "the twelfth apostle"; his supernatural appointment by Christ, it is said, "rebuked the hasty action in the upper room." Paul, however, was never numbered among "the twelve"; nor was James nor Barnabas, who were also called "apostles" (Acts 14:14; Gal. 1:19). Paul was "not a whit behind the very chiefest apostles," yet it was never recorded of him that "he was numbered with the eleven," as it was of him as to whose election the Christians in "the upper room" reasoned and prayed.

Peter is the first to move in the matter; naturally so, as he is always the first to speak and to act; but he claims no authority; he does not appoint a successor to Judas, nor do the eleven apostles unite in electing a successor. The whole body of Christians is consulted; it is significant that just here their number is given as "about a hundred and twenty," as if to indicate that all participated equally in the act. From the very first there is a note of democracy in the government of the church.

The appeal of Peter is to the Old Testament. (Ps. 69:25; 109:8.) Jesus had opened the mind of the disciples "that they might understand the scriptures" (Luke 24:45). The psalmist had in mind, probably, a traitor of his own day, such as Ahithophel; but the words are interpreted as a symbolic prophecy of Judas and his treachery. The authority of the Old Testament is thus recognized, but it is interpreted in the light of the new faith.

As to Judas, the reference to his revolting death (vs. 18-19) is made by Luke, the historian, and is not a part of the speech of Peter. Its apparent discrepancy from the account given in the Gospels can be reconciled, probably, by supposing that the rope used by the suicide broke, and further that the use made of the money which he threw down in the Temple is indicated by the statement that he "obtained a field with the reward of his iniquity." More important is the question as to how he became an apostate and a traitor. The true view of his character and career is not that which makes him either a monster of iniquity or an innocent blunderer. He was neither. His case is painfully familiar. His is the example of one who, in the light of close companionship with Christ, clings to an evil passion. Under such conditions, character most rapidly deteriorates. His love of gain gradually becomes his master, and when circumstances have so combined he is willing, for a few pieces of silver, to betray his Lord. His career is not a study in psychology for the curious; it is a practical warning for every follower of Christ.

The apostolate, as described by Peter, was of the nature of a "bishopric," or an "overseership"; the apostles were to be the official leaders of the Christian community; yet, more important still, they were to be the official witnesses to the life and teachings, and particularly to the resurrection, of Christ. For this reason Peter suggested that, to fill the place of Judas, one should be chosen who had been a companion of Christ and who thus would be a credible witness of the resurrection. Paul was qualified by a supernatural and glorious vision of the risen Lord. In the strict sense, of course, apostles no longer exist; but the principle still holds that while all believers may testify for Christ, the church is wise in selecting and training certain men who as ordained ministers may be official witnesses to the truth.

The choice of Matthias was not merely by a resort to "the lot"; first of all, the disciples exercised their reason, and narrowed down their choice to two men, either of whom was qualified to fill the office; then the final decision was left to the Lord, who was addressed in prayer. Finally, to be certain of his will, "they gave lots for them; and the lot fell upon Matthias." The use of the lot is not always wrong; but it is noticeable that after the Day of Pentecost it is never again mentioned in the New Testament. The Lord guides his followers by his Spirit, but he expects us to reason from providences, to consult Scripture, and, above all else, to submit our wills to his in prayer.

In this story of the election of Matthias, prayer to Christ is first recorded; it is not the last such prayer. Intercession properly may be addressed to the Father or the Son or the Holy Spirit; but the usual form is to the Father, in the name of the Son, by the power of the Spirit. It is evident that Luke wishes us to understand that Matthias was properly chosen and in accordance with the will of Christ. He declares that "he was numbered with the eleven apostles"; and Luke afterward shows how the name of the apostolic band was gradually changed from "the eleven" to "the twelve" (chs. 1:26; 2:14; 6:2). The number of official witnesses is now complete; overseers are ready to care for the new converts. Pentecost will follow, and its events will fill the first great chapter in the history of the church as it witnesses for Christ.

B. THE FIRST CONVERTS Ch. 2

1. THE PENTECOSTAL GIFT   Ch. 2:1-13

1 And when the day of Pentecost was now come, they were all together in one place. 2 And suddenly there came from heaven a sound as of the rushing of a mighty wind, and it filled all the house where they were sitting. 3 And there appeared unto them tongues parting asunder, like as of fire; and it sat upon each one of them. 4 And they were all filled with the Holy Spirit, and began to speak with other tongues, as the Spirit gave them utterance.

5 Now there were dwelling at Jerusalem Jews, devout men, from every nation under heaven. 6 And when this sound was heard, the multitude came together, and were confounded, because that every man heard them speaking in his own language. 7 And they were all amazed and marvelled, saying, Behold, are not all these that speak Galilæans? 8 And how hear we, every man in our own language wherein we were born? 9 Parthians and Medes and Elamites, and the dwellers in Mesopotamia, in Judæa and Cappadocia, in Pontus and Asia, 10 in Phrygia and Pamphylia, in Egypt and the parts of Libya about Cyrene, and sojourners from Rome, both Jews and proselytes, 11 Cretans and Arabians, we hear them speaking in our tongues the mighty works of God. 12 And they were all amazed, and were perplexed, saying one to another, What meaneth this? 13 But others mocking said, They are filled with new wine.

No more opportune day could have been selected for the disciples to begin their witness for Christ; for Pentecost was the most popular feast of the Jewish year and the whole city was then thronged with pilgrims from every quarter of the globe. As the name implies, this feast fell on "the fiftieth day" after the Sabbath of Passover week. It was also called the "Day of First Fruits," for it was a harvest festival, and its observance included the presenting to the Lord of two loaves made from the ripened wheat. Thus there could have been no more fitting time for the first great gathering of converts into the Christian church. Figuratively speaking, this Day of Pentecost has never ended, for by the same power and by the preaching of the same message souls are still being gathered into the garner of God.

This power is that of the Holy Spirit. We are not to imagine that at this Pentecost he first came into the world. In all ages he had been imparting life and guidance and strength and holiness to the people of God; but he was now to work with a new instrument, namely, the truth concerning a crucified, risen, ascended, divine Savior. For the proclamation of this truth the church was the appointed agent; the story of Pentecost, therefore, is the first chapter in the history of the church as it witnesses for Christ, and it embodies the impressive lesson that in all successful witnessing the power is that of the Spirit and the instrument is the message of the gospel.

As the story opens the disciples are assembled, probably in "the upper room," on a Sunday morning, with their hearts fixed upon Christ, waiting for the fulfillment of his promise. Such a place and time and attitude are unfailing conditions of blessing. "Suddenly there came from heaven a sound as of the rushing of a mighty wind"; there was no wind, but the sound was a symbol of the Spirit; it indicated his power, mighty, mysterious, heavenly but unseen. "And there appeared unto them tongues parting asunder, like as of fire; and it sat upon each one of them"; there was no fire, but upon each believer there rested a luminous tongue, symbolic of the fervent, zealous witness each would be empowered to bear. "And they were all filled with the Holy Spirit"; they were brought completely under his control; that was for the disciples the essential experience of Pentecost. It was repeated again and again in the days which followed. It is an experience which is normal and natural for all the followers of Christ. His Spirit never leaves a believer, but ever and again, as one is surrendered to the will of the Lord, he is absolutely, if unconsciously, dominated by his Spirit.

In the case of these disciples the experience was accompanied by a marvelous gift and they "began to speak with other tongues, as the Spirit gave them utterance." This ability to speak in foreign languages not previously learned was merely a temporary endowment granted for a special purpose. It was one of those miraculous spiritual gifts which marked the age of the apostles. In modern times the claim to possess this power has never been established on credible evidence, nor is the dominance of the Spirit in the life of a believer to be tested by the presence of any special gift. One who is obedient to his Master is granted the ability to do the will of the Master, not necessarily in spectacular service but surely in holy living, for "the fruit of the Spirit is love, joy, peace, longsuffering, kindness, goodness, faithfulness, meekness, self-control."

The gift of tongues was exactly the preparation needed by the disciples for the task of witnessing to the throngs who had gathered from all parts of the world to observe the feast; for "there were dwelling at Jerusalem Jews, devout men, from every nation under heaven." The miracles of the Bible were not mere prodigies which aroused wonder; they had a practical purpose. So this gift at Pentecost made it possible for the gospel story to be given on a single day to hearers from many different nations.

Miracles, however, did occasion surprise and arouse interest; for this also they were designed, and the gift of tongues at once drew together a great multitude and fixed their attention upon messages to which otherwise they might have been indifferent, for when "every man heard them speaking in his own language . . . they were all amazed and marvelled."

Miracles, moreover, were "signs" of divine power and symbols of abiding truths. Thus the gift of tongues convinced many hearers of the reality of the gospel message as the disciples declared "the mighty works of God." To others the utterances seemed but the babbling of men who were "filled with new wine"; and thus the story of the cross has often been regarded as "foolishness" by the reputed wise men of the world.

To the disciples the gift of tongues and the providential opportunity of addressing men from so many different countries and nations must have brought the remembrance of the promised presence and power of the Master and of his assurance that they should be his witnesses "unto the uttermost part of the earth." To the church of today this story of the Pentecostal gift should bring a like assurance of needed grace for those who undertake to carry the gospel of Christ to all the peoples of the world.

2. PETER'S FIRST SERMON   Ch. 2:14-41

14 But Peter, standing up with the eleven, lifted up his voice, and spake forth unto them, saying, *Ye men of Judæa, and all ye that dwell at Jerusalem, be this known unto you, and give ear unto my words. 15 For these are not drunken, as ye suppose; seeing it is* but *the third hour of the day; 16 but this is that which hath been spoken through the prophet Joel:*

17 And it shall be in the last days, saith God,
   I will pour forth of my Spirit upon all flesh:
   And your sons and your daughters shall prophesy,
   And your young men shall see visions,
   And your old men shall dream dreams:
18 Yea and on my servants and on my handmaidens in those days
   Will I pour forth of my Spirit; and they shall prophesy.
19 And I will show wonders in the heaven above,
   And signs on the earth beneath;
   Blood, and fire, and vapor of smoke:
20 The sun shall be turned into darkness,
   And the moon into blood,
   Before the day of the Lord come,
   That great and notable day:
21 And it shall be, that whosoever shall call on the name of the Lord shall be saved.

22 Ye men of Israel, hear these words: Jesus of Nazareth, a man approved of God unto you by mighty works and wonders and signs which God did by him in the midst of you, even as ye yourselves know; 23 him, being delivered up by the determinate counsel and foreknowledge of God, ye by the hand of lawless men did crucify and slay: 24 whom God raised up, having loosed the pangs of death: because it was not possible that he should be holden of it. 25 For David saith concerning him,

   I beheld the Lord always before my face;
   For he is on my right hand, that I should not be moved:
26 Therefore my heart was glad, and my tongue rejoiced;
   Moreover my flesh also shall dwell in hope:

27 *Because thou wilt not leave my soul unto Hades,*
Neither wilt thou give thy Holy One to see corruption.
28 *Thou madest known unto me the ways of life;*
Thou shalt make me full of gladness with thy counte-
nance.
29 *Brethren, I may say unto you freely of the patriarch*
David, that he both died and was buried, and his tomb is
with us unto this day. 30 Being therefore a prophet, and
knowing that God had sworn with an oath to him, that of
the fruit of his loins he would set one upon his throne; 31
he foreseeing this spake of the resurrection of the Christ,
that neither was he left unto Hades, nor did his flesh see
corruption. 32 This Jesus did God raise up, whereof we
all are witnesses. 33 Being therefore by the right hand of
God exalted, and having received of the Father the prom-
ise of the Holy Spirit, he hath poured forth this, which ye
see and hear. 34 For David ascended not into the heav-
ens: but he saith himself,
The Lord said unto my Lord,
Sit thou on my right hand,
35 *Till I make thine enemies the footstool of thy feet.*
36 *Let all the house of Israel therefore know assuredly,*
that God hath made him both Lord and Christ, this Jesus
whom ye crucified.
37 *Now when they heard this, they were pricked in their*
heart, and said unto Peter and the rest of the apostles,
Brethren, what shall we do? 38 And Peter said unto them,
Repent ye, and be baptized every one of you in the name
of Jesus Christ unto the remission of your sins; and ye
shall receive the gift of the Holy Spirit. 39 For to you is
the promise, and to your children, and to all that are afar
off, even as many as the Lord our God shall call unto him.
40 *And with many other words he testified, and exhorted*
them, saying, Save yourselves from this crooked genera-
tion. 41 They then that received his word were baptized:
and there were added unto them in that day about three
thousand souls.

The presence and power of the Holy Spirit were manifested at Pentecost not only by the gift of tongues, but
quite as truly by the sermon of Peter which resulted in
the conversion of three thousand souls. How else can be

accounted for the intrepid courage of the man who in cowardice, a few days earlier, had denied his Lord, but who now stands before a multitude in the streets of Jerusalem boldly rebuking a nation for its unbelief and crime? No less astonishing are the skill and wisdom shown by this untutored fisherman as he so marshals his arguments and presents his proofs as to avoid offense and to bring conviction to a hostile and bigoted multitude.

No modern preacher can claim such divine inspiration as Peter enjoyed; yet one who would be used by the Spirit should imitate him in at least two particulars: he preached Christ and he expounded the Scriptures. The purpose of his address was to prove that Jesus of Nazareth is the Messiah, the divine Savior of the world; in demonstrating this theme he used as his proofs Old Testament quotations which indeed comprised nearly half of his sermon.

a. The Introduction (vs. 14-21) shrewdly refers to the gift of tongues, defending the disciples against the charge of intoxication on the ground of Jewish customs, and explaining the miracle as a partial fulfillment of the prophecy of Joel which declared that this present age would be marked by such manifestations of the Spirit's power as Peter declared the gift of tongues to be. Joel had predicted, however, that the age would end amid terrific portents and in divine judgment, but that "whosoever shall call on the name of the Lord shall be saved." That Jesus of Nazareth is the divine Lord who will someday return in judgment, upon whom men must now call in penitence and faith, this is the truth Peter proceeded to establish; and it is the heart of every gospel message today.

b. The Argument (vs. 22-36) is threefold: (1) Jesus had been approved of God by "mighty works and wonders and signs"; of these the hearers were witnesses. In modern days it is not popular to argue from the miracles of Christ to the reality of his claims and to his saving power; but one need not be ashamed to imitate this logic of the apostle Peter.

(2) Jesus died and rose again (vs. 23-32); the Christ, according to Scripture was to die and rise again; therefore Jesus was the Christ. This argument from the resurrection of our Lord is still valid. His victory over death was the greatest of all miracles. Our Christian faith is still based on the facts implied by that empty tomb. This truth is still to be proclaimed as the hope of the world. Of this resurrection Peter declared the disciples were the witnesses; to the same fact of a living Christ all believers should bear testimony by their words and deeds.

(3) Jesus ascended to the "right hand" of God; the Christ, according to the prediction of David, was so to ascend (vs. 34-35); the gift of the Holy Spirit was proof that Jesus thus had assumed the place of supreme power. Therefore this argument, like the two already stated, led to the conclusion that Jesus is indeed the Lord and Christ of whom Joel and other prophets had spoken; and it was at once evident that, in rejecting and crucifying him, the Jews had been guilty of an unparalleled crime. So, too, the present work of the Holy Spirit is a witness to the divine power of Christ, and those who reject Christ are refusing a salvation which he alone can give, and are placing themselves in opposition to the only power which can bring blessing to them and to the world.

c. The Appeal (vs. 37-40), with which Peter closes his sermon, is made to men who have been stirred in their hearts by his presentation of Christ. He pleads with them to repent and to be baptized, and he promises them the gift of the Holy Spirit; for all the blessings which the divine Lord can give are assured to those who turn from sin and sincerely confess their faith in him.

d. The Result of this sermon (v. 41) was the conversion of three thousand souls; this, too, was a manifestation of the power of the Holy Spirit, for, no matter how eloquent or Scriptural the sermon, souls are renewed only by the Spirit of the living Christ.

3. THE LIFE OF THE CONVERTS   Ch. 2:42-47

42 And they continued stedfastly in the apostles' teaching and fellowship, in the breaking of bread and the prayers.
43 And fear came upon every soul: and many wonders and signs were done through the apostles. 44 And all that believed were together, and had all things common; 45 and they sold their possessions and goods, and parted them to all, according as any man had need. 46 And day by day, continuing stedfastly with one accord in the temple, and breaking bread at home, they took their food with gladness and singleness of heart, 47 praising God, and having favor with all the people. And the Lord added to them day by day those that were saved.

No less marvelous than the gift of tongues or the eloquence of Peter or the conversion of a multitude was the conduct of those who accepted Christ as their Savior. Many persons seem to suppose that Pentecostal power is attested by striking gifts or ability in public speech; its best proof is found in the daily life of the believer. These early Christians continued to seek for instruction from the men who really knew the Lord; they rejoiced in spiritual fellowship; they observed the sacrament which reminded them of the Savior's death; they met frequently for prayer and praise; they were cheerful and contented; they loved one another so fervently that "they sold their possessions and goods, and parted them to all, according as any man had need." The Spirit of Christ bound these believers into one body, united in faith and love and hope; and thus it is not strange that Pentecost is commonly regarded as the true birthday of the Christian church; nor is it surprising that such men were held in "favor with all the people" and that additions were made to their numbers "day by day."

C. THE FIRST OPPOSITION Chs. 3:1 to 4:31

1. THE LAME MAN HEALED   Ch. 3:1-10

1 Now Peter and John were going up into the temple at the hour of prayer, being the ninth hour. 2 And a cer-

*tain man that was lame from his mother's womb was car-
ried, whom they laid daily at the door of the temple which
is called Beautiful, to ask alms of them that entered into
the temple; 3 who seeing Peter and John about to go into
the temple, asked to receive an alms.   4 And Peter, fastening his eyes upon him, with John, said, Look on us.
5 And he gave heed unto them, expecting to receive something from them.   6 But Peter said, Silver and gold have
I none; but what I have, that give I thee.   In the name of
Jesus Christ of Nazareth, walk.   7 And he took him by
the right hand, and raised him up: and immediately his
feet and his ankle-bones received strength.   8 And leaping
up, he stood, and began to walk; and he entered with them
into the temple, walking, and leaping, and praising God.
9 And all the people saw him walking and praising God:
10 and they took knowledge of him, that it was he that sat
for alms at the Beautiful Gate of the temple; and they were
filled with wonder and amazement at that which had happened unto him.*

The healing of the lame man at the Beautiful Gate of
the Temple was not the first and possibly not the most
marvelous miracle which had been wrought by the apostles
since the Day of Pentecost; but it is related because it
brought the apostles to the notice of the Jewish rulers and
resulted in the first serious opposition to the Christian
church.   The whole story forms an important section of
The Acts, for in the history of "The Church Witnessing
for Christ" this narrative shows the independence of the
church and its boldness in witnessing.

The recital of the miracle is in itself interesting, instructive, and dramatically vivid.   The agents through whom
the marvel is wrought are Peter and John.   As in the
Gospel narrative they are united in closest fellowship with
Christ, so in The Acts they are companions in the leadership of his church.   These two apostles "were going up into
the temple at the hour of prayer," for, like all their fellow
Christians, they still regarded themselves as loyal Jews and
observed all the ceremonies and forms of their national
worship.   Surely it is well for the people of God always

to have fixed places and times for prayer.

They are about to pass from the outer to the inner courts of the Temple. Their way leads through the gate which was called "Beautiful" because of its superb doors of Corinthian bronze. Their attention is drawn to a poor cripple who has been lame from his birth, who for years has been carried daily to this public place that he might have opportunity "to ask alms of them that entered into the temple." When he makes his appeal to the apostles his hopes are aroused by the reply of Peter, "Look on us."

Then he is startled as he hears the words: "Silver and gold have I none; but what I have, that give I thee. In the name of Jesus Christ of Nazareth, walk." Peter meant, of course, that he had for the man something not less but more valuable than "silver and gold"; he offered to the helpless man healing "in the name" of Christ, that is, in virtue of all that had been revealed and declared concerning Christ as a living, divine Savior. To this promise the faith of the cripple made an instant response. Then Peter "took him by the right hand, and raised him up," not to strengthen his feet but his faith; "and leaping up, he stood, and began to walk; and he entered with them into the temple, walking, and leaping, and praising God. And all the people saw him . . . and they were filled with wonder and amazement." It was indeed a notable cure; the man was well known, there were countless witnesses to identify him, he had been a cripple for forty years, and he was given "perfect soundness" in an instant of time, as he put his trust in the living Christ.

It is not unwise to dwell upon the truths which such a story may symbolize. The human race may be pictured as lying outside the temple of true life, of real service, of actual worship. Weak and helpless and hopeless, mankind is in need of the transforming power which comes to those who put their trust in Christ. Men have less need of alms than of spiritual renewal, less need of charity than of strength for self-support. It is the duty of the church to stretch out the right hand in loving ministry, to offer relief and to express sympathy, but to do so "in the name of Jesus Christ," and to inspire faith in him who alone can heal and save.

2. PETER'S SECOND SERMON   Ch. 3:11-26

11 And as he held Peter and John, all the people ran together unto them in the porch that is called Solomon's, greatly wondering. 12 And when Peter saw it, he answered unto the people, Ye men of Israel, why marvel ye at this man? or why fasten ye your eyes on us, as though by our own power or godliness we had made him to walk? 13 The God of Abraham, and of Isaac, and of Jacob, the God of our fathers, hath glorified his Servant Jesus; whom ye delivered up, and denied before the face of Pilate, when he had determined to release him. 14 But ye denied the Holy and Righteous One, and asked for a murderer to be granted unto you, 15 and killed the Prince of life; whom God raised from the dead; whereof we are witnesses. 16 And by faith in his name hath his name made this man strong, whom ye behold and know: yea, the faith which is through him hath given him this perfect soundness in the presence of you all. 17 And now, brethren, I know that in ignorance ye did it, as did also your rulers. 18 But the things which God foreshowed by the mouth of all the prophets, that his Christ should suffer, he thus fulfilled. 19 Repent ye therefore, and turn again, that your sins may be blotted out, that so there may come seasons of refreshing from the presence of the Lord; 20 and that he may send the Christ who hath been appointed for you, even Jesus: 21 whom the heaven must receive until the times of restoration of all things, whereof God spake by the mouth of his holy prophets that have been from of old. 22 Moses indeed said, A prophet shall the Lord God raise up unto you from among your brethren, like unto me; to him shall ye hearken in all things whatsoever he shall speak unto you. 23 And it shall be, that every soul that shall not hearken to that prophet, shall be utterly destroyed from among the people. 24 Yea and all the prophets

*from Samuel and them that followed after, as many as
have spoken, they also told of these days. 25 Ye are the
sons of the prophets, and of the covenant which God made
with your fathers, saying unto Abraham, And in thy seed
shall all the families of the earth be blessed. 26 Unto
you first God, having raised up his Servant, sent him to
bless you, in turning away every one of you from your
iniquities.*

The notable miracle which had been wrought at the
Beautiful Gate of the Temple provided for Peter an eager
audience, and also afforded him a proof of the truth he
wished to establish. So it had been on the Day of Pentecost; the gift of tongues attracted the attention of a multitude and also established the fact that Jesus was "Lord
and Christ." So when a cripple who had been lame from
his birth was healed in the name of Christ, "all the people
ran together . . . in the porch that is called Solomon's,
greatly wondering." To the throng thus gathered in the
great portico or cloister on the east side of the Temple
area, Peter delivered his second recorded sermon.

a. The Theme (vs. 12-18), as at Pentecost, is the fact
that Jesus is the Christ, the Servant of God, the divine.
Savior. The miracle which had attracted the crowd, as
the miracle at Pentecost, gave to Peter an introduction to
his theme and also its supreme demonstration. Pointing
to the man who had been healed, Peter declares that the
marvel had been producd by no power of his own but by
faith in Jesus; it was this faith which had given to the
cripple "this perfect soundness." This Jesus had been
"delivered up" and "killed"; but such a miracle of healing, wrought by no human wisdom, was a certain proof
that he had risen from the dead, and was manifesting his
divine presence and power.

In thus witnessing for his divine Lord, Peter also sets
forth the incomparable crime of those by whom he had
been rejected and crucified. This charge is made the more
emphatic by a series of striking verbal contrasts. In their

guilty unbelief they had really rejected the God of their
fathers whom they professed to serve. They delivered to
death One whom even the pagan Pilate would have released. They "denied the Holy and Righteous One, and
asked for a murderer." They chose a destroyer of life in
place of the giver and "Prince of life." Him whom they
killed, God raised up. He whom they regarded as a male-
factor had wrought this marvelous benefaction. The miracle was a vindication of Jesus, but it convicted those who
had refused to accept him.

Peter makes two additional statements; neither excuses
his hearers, but both give them hope of pardon. First,
they had acted in ignorance; it was sinful, but might be
pardoned should they now repent in the light of the testimony concerning a risen Christ. Second, the death of
Christ, which they had secured, was part of the plan of
salvation of which all the prophets had spoken; this did
not mitigate their crime, but it declared to them the divine
provision for the forgiveness of sin.

b. A Call to Repentance (vs. 19-21) naturally follows.
It is brief and serious, yet it is enforced by no threat, but
based upon most gracious promises. These point to blessings both individual and universal, both for the immediate
present and for the distant future. If they would sincerely
repent of their unbelief and would turn from their evil
ways, their sins would be "blotted out"; and, more marvelous still, Jesus Christ would come back again from
heaven and the whole world would experience the glad
"times of restoration" of which all the poets and prophets
have sung. Forgiveness of sins has been made possible by
the first coming of Christ, by his sufferings and death; but
universal blessing is conditioned upon his appearing a
second time. Every repentant believer is hastening that
day, and such messages as this of Peter lead men to repentance.

c. An Appeal to Scripture (vs. 22-26) closes the sermon and bases both its warnings and its promises upon

the words of Moses and the prophets. Even the great law-giver had specifically predicted the coming of Christ and had declared the doom of all who refuse to accept him: "Every soul that shall not hearken to that prophet, shall be utterly destroyed." However, "all the prophets from Samuel" had foretold the present days of grace; they had spoken of the atoning work of Christ, and of his coming glory; the promises of blessing were for "all the families of the earth," but first of all the offer of salvation had come to Israel; to them the Christ had been sent to bless them in turning every one from his sins. The same Savior is being presented today, and his appointed messengers declare his pardoning grace, the peril of rejecting him, and the possibility of sharing the blessedness of his perfected Kingdom.

3. THE BOLDNESS OF PETER AND JOHN   Ch. 4:1-22

1 And as they spake unto the people, the priests and the captain of the temple and the Sadducees came upon them, 2 being sore troubled because they taught the people, and proclaimed in Jesus the resurrection from the dead. 3 And they laid hands on them, and put them in ward unto the morrow: for it was now eventide. 4 But many of them that heard the word believed; and the number of the men came to be about five thousand.

5 And it came to pass on the morrow, that their rulers and elders and scribes were gathered together in Jerusalem; 6 and Annas the high priest was there, and Caiaphas, and John, and Alexander, and as many as were of the kindred of the high priest. 7 And when they had set them in the midst, they inquired, By what power, or in what name, have ye done this? 8 Then Peter, filled with the Holy Spirit, said unto them, Ye rulers of the people, and elders, 9 if we this day are examined concerning a good deed done to an impotent man, by what means this man is made whole; 10 be it known unto you all, and to all the people of Israel, that in the name of Jesus Christ of Nazareth, whom ye crucified, whom God raised from the dead, even

*in him doth this man stand here before you whole. 11 He
is the stone which was set at nought of you the builders,
which was made the head of the corner. 12 And in none
other is there salvation: for neither is there any other
name under heaven, that is given among men, wherein we
must be saved. 13 Now when they beheld the boldness
of Peter and John, and had perceived that they were unlearned and ignorant men, they marvelled; and they took
knowledge of them, that they had been with Jesus.
14 And seeing the man that was healed standing with them,
they could say nothing against it. 15 But when they had
commanded them to go aside out of the council, they conferred among themselves, 16 saying, What shall we do to
these men? for that indeed a notable miracle hath been
wrought through them, is manifest to all that dwell in Jerusalem; and we cannot deny it. 17 But that it spread no
further among the people, let us threaten them, that they
speak henceforth to no man in this name. 18 And they
called them, and charged them not to speak at all nor teach
in the name of Jesus. 19 But Peter and John answered
and said unto them, Whether it is right in the sight of God
to hearken unto you rather than unto God, judge ye:
20 for we cannot but speak the things which we saw and
heard. 21 And they, when they had further threatened
them, let them go, finding nothing how they might punish
them, because of the people; for all men glorified God for
that which was done. 22 For the man was more than
forty years old, on whom this miracle of healing was
wrought.*

a. The Arrest of the Apostles (vs. 1-4) was due not so
much to the miracle which they had wrought as to the
claims of which the miracle had been the occasion and
the proof. It was the sermon of Peter which aroused the
antagonism of the rulers and resulted in the first opposition to the Christian church. These rulers were prompt
to act. While the apostles were still addressing the crowd
which the miracle had attracted, "the priests and the captain of the temple and the Sadducees came upon them
. . . and put them in ward unto the morrow." "The

captain of the temple," the priest who was in charge of the sacred precincts, may have feared a tumult when he saw the excitement aroused by the man who had been healed; but the secret source of the opposition is disclosed by the mention of the "Sadducees." They were the real instigators of the movement. They formed the most aristocratic, wealthy, and powerful party in Jerusalem, but also the least orthodox. As they were materialists and denied the doctrines of a future life and of the immortality of the soul, they were "sore troubled" because the apostles "taught the people, and proclaimed in Jesus the resurrection from the dead." It must have angered them to be told that the man whom they had crucified had risen and was again to appear. It may also be noticed that they would be jealous of any popular movement which might lessen their power and endanger the rich revenues they reaped from the Temple worship. However, their action was cautious and guarded. They merely secured the arrest of the apostles, who were placed in confinement, only to be detained until the next day because the hour was now too late for a public trial.

It should be observed that skeptics like the Sadducees have always been the most bitter enemies of Christ; further that the attacks upon the church became more bitter only as its members were better prepared to endure the trial; and further that the church always thrives under persecution. This is the significance, possibly, of the surprising connection of the statements that Peter and John were arrested, and that "many of them that heard the word believed; and the number of the men come to be about five thousand."

b. The Arraignment of Peter and John (vs. 5-7) formed an imposing scene. The "rulers and elders and scribes were gathered together," that is, there was a session of the Sanhedrin, the highest court of the nation. Among its members were Annas, who had been deposed by the Romans but was still regarded as high priest by the Jews;

Caiaphas, his son-in-law, who had been appointed as his successor; and John and Alexander, whose names are mentioned to add to the impression of the dignity and power and representative character of the council.

The question officially addressed to the disciples was not sincere, but was intended as a snare to draw from them an answer which might be construed technically as blasphemy: "By what power [in yourselves], or in what name [of magic or incantation] have ye done this?" They hoped that the apostles would ascribe divine power to some being other than God. Their implied challenge was at once accepted; and the apostles declared the miracle to have been wrought by their divine Savior and Lord.

c. The Answer of the Apostles (vs. 8-12) is characterized, however, by marked courtesy and dignity. When men of humble station are faced by such an august tribunal they usually exhibit either cringing cowardice or brazen insolence. Peter is courteous; but we cannot fail to notice the sarcasm of his opening sentence: "If we . . . are examined concerning a good deed done to an impotent man"—if this is the case, is it not absurd to treat as criminals men who have merely relieved distress? Thus Peter at once places in a ridiculous light his enemies who in cowardice and treachery have asked an explanation of the miracle. Yet he proceeds to answer their question, and rejoices in the fact that his judges do not and cannot deny the reality of the miracle or separate it from the testimony which he is ready to bear. He boldly declares that the man has been healed in the name of Jesus Christ, whom these rulers killed, whom in striking contrast "God raised from the dead"; they had treated him with contempt, but God had raised him to the place of supreme honor—"a stone . . . set at nought," but now "made the head of the corner." "Neither is there any other name under heaven, that is given among men, wherein we must be saved," thus Peter asserts not only that the miracle has been wrought in the name of Jesus Christ, but that he and his judges can have eternal salvation in no other name. His words are at once a rebuke, a challenge, and an invitation. They need to be reviewed and weighed today by certain benevolent but superficial talkers who are asserting that Christianity is only one among many religions, and that it is only necessary for one to be sincere in his own belief. Such teachers must reconcile their statements with those of Peter and John who were "filled with the Holy Spirit" when they declared that there is but one Name wherein we must be saved.

d. The Threat of the Rulers and the Calm Defiance of the Apostles (vs. 13-22) not only emphasize further the courage of Peter and John but also actually mark a crisis in the history of the church. For two reasons the boldness of the apostles astonished the members of the council. First, they were "unlearned and ignorant men," which does not mean that they were illiterate, but that they had not received the technical training of the Jewish schools and therefore might not have dared to dispute with the skilled lawyers who composed the court. Second, "they took knowledge of them, that they had been with Jesus"; this familiar statement is usually taken to mean that the knowledge explained the conduct of the apostles; on the other hand, it really added to the perplexity of the rulers; the apostles "had been with Jesus," they knew him intimately, they could not have been mistaken easily as to his identity, yet they declared him to be alive, and in spite of their humble rank they insisted, even before the Sanhedrin, that Jesus was living and that miracles were being wrought in his name.

The rulers held a secret conference; they could not deny the miracle, for the man who had been healed was standing in their midst, but they could forbid the apostles to "teach in the name of Jesus." This they did with severe threatenings; and they received the memorable reply: "Whether it is right in the sight of God to hearken unto you rather than unto God, judge ye: for we cannot but

speak the things which we saw and heard." By these
words the apostles virtually declared the church to be independent of the Jewish state, and they repudiated the
rulers as being opposed to God on whose side the apostles
claimed to be. Peter and John may not have seen the full
significance of their words; but their bold determination to
witness for Christ was the first great step in the development of the church from a Jewish sect into a universal
brotherhood. It does require courage to separate from
associations which one has held sacred and to oppose authorities whom one has regarded as supreme; but the only
possible course for a Christian is the one which he believes
to be "right in the sight of God." Such a choice always
results in larger liberties and increased power.

4. The Prayer of the Church   Ch. 4:23-31

*23 And being let go, they came to their own company,
and reported all that the chief priests and the elders had
said unto them. 24 And they, when they heard it, lifted
up their voice to God with one accord, and said, O Lord,
thou that didst make the heaven and the earth and the sea,
and all that in them is: 25 who by the Holy Spirit, by the
mouth of our father David thy servant, didst say,*

Why did the Gentiles rage,

And the peoples imagine vain things?

26 The kings of the earth set themselves in array,

And the rulers were gathered together,

Against the Lord, and against his Anointed:

*27 for of a truth in this city against thy holy Servant Jesus,
whom thou didst anoint, both Herod and Pontius Pilate,
with the Gentiles and the peoples of Israel, were gathered
together, 28 to do whatsoever thy hand and thy counsel
foreordained to come to pass. 29 And now, Lord, look
upon their threatenings: and grant unto thy servants to
speak thy word with all boldness, 30 while thou stretchest
forth thy hand to heal; and that signs and wonders may be
done through the name of thy holy Servant Jesus. 31 And
when they had prayed, the place was shaken wherein they*

were gathered together; and they were all filled with the Holy Spirit, and thy spake the word of God with boldness.

When Peter and John were released by the rulers, they hastened back to their fellow Christians to report their experiences. A meeting was held for praise and prayer. There was rejoicing in the deliverance of the apostles and in the bold witness they had been called to bear; but the situation was serious. They were commissioned to witness for Christ, and now the supreme rulers of the nation had positively forbidden all testimony in his name. Their minds turned for comfort to the Scriptures, that unfailing source of consolation to Christians in all ages. It was the Second Psalm which brought them the needed message; in all ages the gift of sacred song pours its balm on sore hearts in hours of need. In the words of David they found a description of the opposition offered to Christ, and now to his church. The parallel is perfect; the psalmist had spoken of " kings" and "rulers" and "Gentiles" and "peoples" arrayed against the "Anointed," and thus Herod the king and Pilate the ruler and the unbelieving "Gentiles" and the "peoples of Israel" set themselves against Jesus, the anointed Christ. As in their prayer the disciples quoted this psalm, they thus identified themselves with their Lord; the same hostility from which he suffered was being directed toward them, his followers. But there is a further implication; the psalm declared that at such opposition, "He that sitteth in the heavens will laugh: the Lord will have them in derision," therefore, as the disciples cry out in their time of need it is to One who can deliver. It was not for deliverance, however, that the disciples made specific request, but for "boldness" in witnessing for Christ and for miracles to accompany and to attest their message. The church of the present day need not expect freedom from opposition; but in all circumstances courage can be shown and wonders can be wrought by those who look to God for help to accomplish their allotted tasks.

The answer is sure to come, as it did to the disciples of old: "The place was shaken wherein they were gathered together; and they were all filled with the Holy Spirit, and they spake the word of God with boldness." The experience has been called "a second Pentecost"; and such indeed it was. Instead, however, of the sound like a wind and the tongues of fire there was a trembling of the ground, to symbolize a divine presence and power. Instead of ability to speak foreign languages, courage was given to testify for Christ before their own countrymen. Christians need to be "filled with the Holy Spirit" again and again. The supreme condition is surrender to Christ and a wholehearted desire to do his will in spite of peril and opposition and hatred. The result will be new courage and power in service, and not infrequently it will come when believers are assembled in some "upper room" where they have met to read the Scriptures, to sing, and to unite their hearts in prayer.

D. THE FIRST DISCIPLINE Chs. 4:32 to 5:11

32 And the multitude of them that believed were of one heart and soul: and not one of them said that aught of the things which he possessed was his own; but they had all things common. 33 And with great power gave the apostles their witness of the resurrection of the Lord Jesus: and great grace was upon them all. 34 For neither was there among them any that lacked: for as many as were possessors of lands or houses sold them, and brought the prices of the things that were sold, 35 and laid them at the apostles' feet: and distribution was made unto each, according as any one had need. 36 And Joseph, who by the apostles was surnamed Barnabas (which is, being interpreted, Son of exhortation), a Levite, a man of Cyprus by race, 37 having a field, sold it, and brought the money and laid it at the apostles' feet.

1 But a certain man named Ananias, with Sapphira, his wife, sold a possession, 2 and kept back part of the price, his wife also being privy to it, and brought a certain part, and laid it at the apostles' feet. 3 But Peter said, Ananias, why hath Satan filled thy heart to lie to the Holy Spirit, and to keep back part of the price of the land? 4 While it remained, did it not remain thine own? and after it was sold, was it not in thy power? How is it that thou hast conceived this thing in thy heart? thou hast not lied unto men, but unto God. 5 And Ananias hearing these words fell down and gave up the ghost: and great fear came upon all that heard it. 6 And the young men arose and wrapped him round, and they carried him out and buried him.

7 And it was about the space of three hours after, when his wife, not knowing what was done, came in. 8 And Peter answered unto her, Tell me whether ye sold the land for so much. And she said, Yea, for so much. 9 But Peter said unto her, How is it that ye have agreed together to try the Spirit of the Lord? behold, the feet of them that have buried thy husband are at the door, and they shall carry thee out. 10 And she fell down immediately at his feet, and gave up the ghost: and the young men came in and found her dead, and they carried her out and buried her by her husband. 11 And great fear came upon the whole church, and upon all that heard these things.

The sin of Ananias and Sapphira found its occasion in the "community of goods" which for a time was practiced by the church in Jerusalem. The custom is first mentioned in connection with the manifestation of the Holy Spirit at Pentecost; so this second reference immediately follows the account of the new infilling of the Spirit experienced by the disciples as they met in prayer. The custom is here more fully explained. It might seem at first that the entire church membership had a common purse, and from this narrative many have argued for "communism" as being truly Christian and apostolic. A more careful reading of all the statements shows that the "community of goods" here described was purely local, temporary, occasional, and voluntary. It was practiced only in Jerusalem, not in other cities of the Empire, and there only for a time. It was not observed by all Chris-

tians even in Jerusalem, in the sense that all their possessions were sold and placed in a common fund. Mary, the
mother of Mark, continued to own her spacious home in
the city and to use it for the entertainment of her Christian
friends. Her nephew, Barnabas, is cited in this paragraph
as an example of special generosity for selling a field which
he owned, and offering the proceeds for the use of the
church. Peter tells Ananias that he had been under no
compulsion to sell his plot of land, and that when it was
sold he had been free to retain the money, if he had so
wished. The facts seem to be that many Christians did
contribute to the treasury of the church all they had, others
sold their possessions from time to time as special demands
for relief arose, still others retained the ownership of their
property regarding it as a sacred trust. The matter was
rather one of sentiment, of spirit, of charity, than of definite requirement and inflexible rule. These believers
"were of one heart and soul," that is the important point;
and when any necessity arose they were quite willing to sell
houses and lands and to place the money "at the apostles'
feet" that distribution might be made "according as any
one had need." From this paragraph, therefore, it is not
well to argue against the right of private ownership today,
nor to seek to establish any particular economic theory.
What is truly significant, remarkable, admirable, is the
love which prompted these believers, so that "not one of
them said that aught of the things which he possessed was
his own." Such an attitude of mind is possible for one
who still retains legal title to the wealth which he is ad-
ministering for the benefit of dependents, and for the good
of the community, the church, and the state. Such love,
however, is the gift of the Spirit, as is suggested by the
connection in which this community of goods is mentioned,
and it is possessed by those who have yielded themselves
wholly to Christ. It may be manifested in some such form
of voluntary communism as was practiced by this early
church; where it exists it is sure to be shown; and where

such true and practical and compelling love for fellow
Christians is seen by the unbelieving world, there, as in
Jerusalem in the early days of the church, the witness of
believers to "the resurrection of the Lord Jesus" will be
attended "with great power."

This voluntary community of goods gave opportunity
for the exhibition of liberality and love, but it also was
open to abuse, to deception, and to fraud. Barnabas, of
Cyprus, is mentioned as a marked illustration of the
former, though why his gift was specially remarkable is
a matter of conjecture; of the latter, and in striking contrast to Barnabas, was the example of Ananias and Sapphira. The weakness of most theories which advocate
communism in any form lies in their presupposing honesty
and generosity, while failing to reckon with human selfish-
ness and depravity.

The sin which appeared first in the early church was
grievous and was visited with the severest punishment, yet
its form is not so unfamiliar today as to lose its lesson of
warning for even the professed followers of Christ. The
offense is commonly regarded as that of lying, and surely
it was that, even though it included many other elements.
Ananias acted a lie, his wife spoke one. He sold a piece
of property and brought to Peter, for the church treasury,
part of the price, pretending that it was the whole. When
Sapphira appeared, Peter asked her whether the amount
brought by her husband was all that had been received
for the land, and she falsely declared that it was. Here it
might be well to pause in the story to observe how painfully common are various kinds of deception and pretense
and affectation and falsehood, and further to suggest a
review of the warnings against this sin which are found
in the Old Testament and in the New. However, Ananias
was not only a liar; he was a thief. This is the meaning
of Peter when he accuses him of having "kept back" dis-
honestly, or having fraudulently concealed, part of the
price. He was guilty, moreover, of impiety and sacrilege.

He had lied not only to men but to God, and actually he had endeavored to rob God, for he had tried to deceive the church which the Holy Spirit was controlling; he had kept for himself part of the sum which he professed to have devoted to a sacred use. Thus the crime is characterized by Peter as an endeavor "to lie to the Holy Spirit" and "to try the Spirit of the Lord." The latter phrase seems to suggest a rash testing of the knowledge and holiness and justice and power of God.

The motives which led to such dishonesty and presumption were probably love of money and love of praise. The former appears in both its common forms of avarice and covetousness. At a time when sacrifice and generosity were expected, Ananias wished to retain his wealth; and by pretending to give to the church all he possessed, he expected henceforth to draw continually upon the fund provided for the poor. Then, too, there was the vain ambition to be regarded as liberal and heroic without the willingness to pay the price. Their obedience to such impulses and their compact in sin show Ananias and Sapphira to have been unbelievers and hypocrites.

Thus it is not difficult to understand the startling severity of the punishment which was visited upon the offenders. By a direct visitation of divine power they were smitten with instant death. God was determined to protect his church from impostors and intruders, so we read that consequently "of the rest durst no man join himself to them." The effect upon the believers was notable also: "Great fear came upon the whole church." It is significant to notice that this is the first time the word "church" appears in The Acts. The connection seems to emphasize the supreme lesson of the story, namely, that the church as a body witnessing for Christ must be kept pure and holy; and it might be added that in no way is consecration more fairly tested than by the practice of individual Christians in the matter of tithes and offerings.

E. THE FIRST PERSECUTION Ch. 5:12-42

By an act of severe discipline God had protected the church from corruption within; he now stretches forth his hand to deliver the church in peril from without. At an earlier period Peter and John had come into collision with the Jewish rulers and had been imprisoned and threatened; but now more severe opposition is experienced: not only two, but all the apostles are arrested; they are not only threatened, but beaten. This was the first real persecution of the Christian church.

1. THE OCCASION Ch. 5:12-16

12 And by the hands of the apostles were many signs and wonders wrought among the people; and they were all with one accord in Solomon's porch. 13 But of the rest durst no man join himself to them: howbeit the people magnified them; 14 and believers were the more added to the Lord, multitudes both of men and women; 15 insomuch that they even carried out the sick into the streets, and laid them on beds and couches, that, as Peter came by, at the least his shadow might overshadow some one of them. 16 And there also came together the multitude from the cities round about Jerusalem, bringing sick folk, and them that were vexed with unclean spirits: and they were healed every one.

The occasion for persecuting the church was found in the rapid growth in the number of believers, and the consequent bitter envy of the Sadducees. This growth was due in no small measure to the extraordinary miracles wrought by the apostles, and to the testimony, which these miracles accredited, which was borne by the apostles in the most public manner as the Christians met daily in Solomon's porch within the precincts of the Temple. So astonishing were the miracles that the news of them spread through every quarter of the sacred city, and the sick were carried out into the streets with the hope that even the shadow of Peter falling on them might effect cures. The excitement spread even outside of Jerusalem, and from the neighboring cities were brought the sick and demon-possessed, and they were healed.

2. IMPRISONMENT AND DELIVERANCE   Ch. 5:17-25

17 But the high priest rose up, and all they that were with him (which is the sect of the Sadducees), and they were filled with jealousy, 18 and laid hands on the apostles, and put them in public ward. 19 But an angel of the Lord by night opened the prison doors, and brought them out, and said, 20 Go ye, and stand and speak in the temple to the people all the words of this Life. 21 And when they heard this, they entered into the temple about daybreak, and taught. But the high priest came, and they that were with him, and called the council together, and all the senate of the children of Israel, and sent to the prison-house to have them brought. 22 But the officers that came found them not in the prison; and they returned, and told, 23 saying, The prison-house we found shut in all safety, and the keepers standing at the doors: but when we had opened, we found no man within. 24 Now when the captain of the temple and the chief priests heard these words, they were much perplexed concerning them whereunto this would grow. 25 And there came one and told them, Behold, the men whom ye put in the prison are in the temple standing and teaching the people.

The imprisonment and the deliverance of the apostles are narrated with dramatic vividness. The Jewish rulers, whose threats have been disregarded, mad with jealousy and hatred, seize the apostles "and put them in public ward," intending to bring them to trial and to death; but by night an angel of the Lord opens the doors and sends the prisoners to preach in the Temple the gospel message which is beautifully designated as "the words of this Life," the good news of the life that is life indeed. It is hardly

wise to deny the agency of angels or to question a supernatural occurrence in this chapter of miracles. Probably
most Christians would do well to believe more implicitly
in the protecting power of those "ministering spirits" which
are "sent forth to do service for the sake of them that shall
inherit salvation." Evidently no other explanation was
given to the Jewish council by the officers who reported
the disappearance of the prisoners; and it is certain that
the wonder and distress of this council were in no measure
relieved when word was brought that the apostles were in
the Temple teaching the people.

3. THE SECOND ARREST   Ch. 5:26-32

*26 Then went the captain with the officers, and brought
them, but without violence; for they feared the people, lest
they should be stoned. 27 And when they had brought
them, they set them before the council. And the high
priest asked them, 28 saying, We strictly charged you not
to teach in this name: and behold, ye have filled Jerusalem
with your teaching, and intend to bring this man's blood
upon us. 29 But Peter and the apostles answered and said,
We must obey God rather than men. 30 The God of our
fathers raised up Jesus, whom ye slew, hanging him on a
tree. 31 Him did God exalt with his right hand to be a
Prince and a Saviour, to give repentance to Israel, and
remission of sins. 32 And we are witnesses of these things;
and so is the Holy Spirit, whom God hath given to them
that obey him.*

When the apostles are again arrested and arraigned, the
reproof of the rulers and the reply of the apostles indicate
the helpless anxiety of the former and the calm confidence
of the latter. The judges take the place of accused criminals, and complain that the followers of Jesus are attempting to bring upon them the responsibility for his death.
The answer of Peter startles them. He boldly charges them
with murder for having secured the crucifixion of Jesus;

but he declares that Jesus has risen, that he occupies the place of supreme power, and that through his name pardon can be secured for those who repent; as witnesses to these truths he declares that the apostles are one with the Holy Spirit. Most startling of all is the bold word: "We must obey God rather than men." Thus he places on one side the chief council of the Jews, and on the other God and the followers of Christ. Here is not only a defiance of his judges; here again is a bold declaration that the Christian church is independent of the Jewish state.

4. THE DEFENSE OF GAMALIEL   Ch. 5:33-39

33 But they, when they heard this, were cut to the heart, and were minded to slay them. 34 But there stood up one in the council, a Pharisee, named Gamaliel, a doctor of the law, had in honor of all the people, and commanded to put the men forth a little while. 35 And he said unto them, Ye men of Israel, take heed to yourselves as touching these men, what ye are about to do. 36 For before these days rose up Theudas, giving himself out to be somebody; to whom a number of men, about four hundred, joined themselves: who was slain; and all, as many as obeyed him, were dispersed, and came to nought. 37 After this man rose up Judas of Galilee in the days of the enrolment, and drew away some of the people after him: he also perished; and all, as many as obeyed him, were scattered abroad. 38 And now I say unto you, Refrain from these men, and let them alone: for if this counsel or this work be of men, it will be overthrown: 39 but if it is of God, ye will not be able to overthrow them; lest haply ye be found even to be fighting against God.

The defense of Gamaliel somewhat abated the wrath of the rulers, and it probably saved the lives of the apostles. Gamaliel was a Pharisee of wide repute and recognized ability. Even with a council composed largely of Sadducees his words carried conviction and largely determined the decision reached. He counseled inaction, delay, caution: "Refrain from these men, and let them alone: for if this counsel or this work be of men, it will be overthrown: but if it is of God, ye will not be able to overthrow them; lest haply ye be found even to be fighting against God." He argued from two historic examples of popular uprisings which had utterly failed, those of Theudas and Judas, both of whom not many years before had appealed to the national hopes of the Jews, had attempted to rebel against the power of Rome, and had perished miserably. Such too, argued Gamaliel, would be the fate of the apostles unless, perchance, they were bearers of a divine message. This counsel was not perfect; it was not wholly courageous; it did not propose an effort to weigh evidence and to discover truth; but it was far from the mad intolerance which had swayed the Jewish court. It rebuked the impatience which so often is the essence of persecution and bigotry. It allowed time to test the right of the cause. Such advice is often needed; it is always infinitely better than a resort to violence, or than the suggestion that might makes right.

5. PUNISHMENT AND LIBERATION   Ch. 5:40-42

40 And to him they agreed: and when they had called the apostles unto them, they beat them and charged them not to speak in the name of Jesus, and let them go. 41 They therefore departed from the presence of the council, rejoicing that they were counted worthy to suffer dishonor for the Name. 42 And every day, in the temple and at home, they ceased not to teach and to preach Jesus as the Christ.

Only in part was Gamaliel's suggestion followed by the Jewish Sanhedrin. They decided to set the apostles free, but they first threatened them and inflicted upon them a cruel beating. It was probably the first physical suffering which had been endured by the followers of Christ. The apostles were undaunted; they rejoiced that they were

counted worthy to suffer dishonor for the name of their
Lord; they boldly continued their testimony, for by his
divine intervention God had set his approval on their
declaration of freedom from the Jewish state, and had assured them of his power and purpose to deliver the church
as it bore its witness for Christ.

F. The First Organization   Ch. 6:1-7

*1 Now in these days, when the number of the disciples
was multiplying, there arose a murmuring of the Grecian
Jews against the Hebrews, because their widows were
neglected in the daily ministration. 2 And the twelve
called the multitude of the disciples unto them, and said, It
is not fit that we should forsake the word of God, and
serve tables. 3 Look ye out therefore, brethren, from
among you seven men of good report, full of the Spirit
and of wisdom, whom we may appoint over this business.
4 But we will continue stedfastly in prayer, and in the ministry of the word. 5 And the saying pleased the whole
multitude: and they chose Stephen, a man full of faith and
of the Holy Spirit, and Philip, and Prochorus, and Ni-
canor, and Timon, and Parmenas, and Nicolaus a prose-
lyte of Antioch; 6 whom they set before the apostles: and
when they had prayed, they laid their hands upon them.
7 And the word of God increased; and the number of
the disciples multiplied in Jerusalem exceedingly; and a
great company of the priests were obedient to the faith.*

The first difficulty within the early church appeared in
connection with the distribution of the fund for the relief
of the poor. "There arose a murmuring" of the Greek-
speaking Jewish Christians against those that spoke Hebrew, the charge being that "their widows were neglected
in the daily ministration." The complaint was probably
well founded, yet the difficulty was due to no intentional
fault, for the condition was not met by punishing offenders
or suggesting more equality in the daily distribution, but
by giving more help to the apostles who were responsible

for the task. The work had grown too burdensome; "the number of the disciples multiplied"; and among the many who needed relief, widows who had no one to represent them, and who could not speak Hebrew, might most naturally be overlooked. However, it does appear that the Greek-speaking Christians were suspicious and that serious trouble threatened.

The apostles showed great wisdom in meeting the difficulty; they called a meeting of the church and advised the election of seven men to whom might be entrusted the task of overseeing the poor. Thus at the very start the government of the church is seen to be democratic; it was not that of a clerical despotism, but of a Christian republic. The election was by the people, but the new officers were ordained by the apostles, who prayed and laid their hands upon them, to indicate that they were solemnly appointed to their new task. Again it should be noted that a distinction is drawn between the officers of the church; one class was to "serve tables," to administer the finances and to care for the needy; the other was to devote itself to preaching and prayer. This regulation as to the ministry of the church shows how church government developed, not by establishing in advance an elaborate system of rules and offices, but by free determination by which new conditions were met as they arose.

The suggestion of the apostles further indicates the character of men who are qualified to serve as officers in the church, even though their ministry is to be concerned with finances and temporal affairs. They were to be "men of good report, full of the Spirit and of wisdom." Integrity and sagacity were not enough; spirituality was likewise required.

The election resulted in the choice of seven men, all of whom bore Greek names. This is no proof, however, that all were Greeks, as such names were common among the Jews and were found in the list of the twelve apostles. It may indicate, however, that most of them were Greek-speaking and were chosen to please the party which had felt aggrieved.

The effect of this new regulation was at once manifested in the more rapid growth of the church. This was due to the spirit of harmony which had been produced, and further to the fact that the apostles were now freed from burdensome details and were able to devote themselves wholly to the preaching of the gospel. Even "a great company of the priests" believed. These men had most of all to lose by their change of faith, and their conversion most forcibly emphasized the swift advance of the Christian cause.

It is quite probable that this incident is the origin of the office of "deacon." The "seven" are not so designated, but their duties seem to have been those performed by deacons in the early history of the church, and it is natural to conclude that this important form of Christian service was first organized at this time.

The paragraph is full of suggestion for the guidance of such officers and also for all who are interested in the matter of church benevolence:

(1) It is the obvious duty of the church, in all places, to provide for its needy members. (2) This provision requires discrimination and care lest the most worthy may be neglected. (3) The administration of relief should include personal contact and sympathy, and should not be merely mechanical and institutional. It should comfort and if possible lead to self-support. (4) This work demands the appointment of special officers. The "minister" must be relieved of details connected with the raising and expending of funds. (5) The minister must be allowed to spend his time in study, in preaching, and in prayer. (6) Relief of the poor, or social service of any kind, can never take the place of evangelistic effort. (7) All church officers are in a true sense "ministers" or "servants," and not lords or masters in the church; and whatever the form of their service, they should seek to bear testimony for Christ, as is suggested by the stories of Stephen and Philip,

two deacons whose public witness forms a significant part of the history which immediately follows.

G. THE FIRST MARTYRDOM Chs. 6:8 to 8:3

1. THE ARREST AND ACCUSATION OF STEPHEN
Ch. 6:8-15

8 And Stephen, full of grace and power, wrought great wonders and signs among the people. 9 But there arose certain of them that were of the synagogue called the synagogue of the Libertines, and of the Cyrenians, and of the Alexandrians, and of them of Cilicia and Asia, disputing with Stephen. 10 And they were not able to withstand the wisdom and the Spirit by which he spake. 11 Then they suborned men, who said, We have heard him speak blasphemous words against Moses, and against God. 12 And they stirred up the people, and the elders, and the scribes, and came upon him, and seized him, and brought him into the council, 13 and set up false witnesses, who said, This man ceaseth not to speak words against this holy place, and the law: 14 for we have heard him say, that this Jesus of Nazareth shall destroy this place, and shall change the customs which Moses delivered unto us. 15 And all that sat in the council, fastening their eyes on him, saw his face as it had been the face of an angel.

The election of "deacons" brought into prominence one whose Greek culture and sympathies aided him in overcoming the narrow prejudices of Judaism and in realizing the universal character of Christianity. Stephen had been appointed to care for needy believers in order that the apostles might be unhampered in their work of preaching; yet his own public witness for Christ was so bold, so clear, so convincing, that it was sealed by martyrdom and marked an epoch in the history of the church. The story of this "layman" emphasizes the truth that the evangelization of the world can never be accomplished by ordained "ministers," unless their testimony is supplemented by that of all members of the church according to their ability and opportunity.

The character of Stephen is clearly sketched; he was "of good report, full of the Spirit and of wisdom"; again, he was "a man full of faith and of the Holy Spirit"; he was "full of grace and power." This "power" manifested itself in the working of "great wonders and signs among the people," but it was also evidenced by his burning eloquence and his skill in argument. The latter was shown as he "disputed" concerning Christ with men of his own race, who opposed his testimony, as he spoke in their place of worship. This was in "the synagogue of the Libertines, and of the Cyrenians, and of the Alexandrians, and of them of Cilicia and Asia." The "Libertines" were descendants of Jews who had been carried captive to Rome a century earlier and afterward made "freedmen." The Cyrenians and the Alexandrians came from North Africa; Cilicia and Asia were provinces of modern Asia Minor. The Grecian Jews, when they came from their various places to reside in Jerusalem, built for themselves one of the many synagogues in the Holy City. The mention of Cilicia is most significant of all; its capital was Tarsus, and from that city there was now in Jerusalem a young Pharisee named Saul. It is almost certain that Saul encountered Stephen in the synagogue, and that meeting affected both his own life and the history of the world.

Whoever the leaders in this synagogue may have been, as they opposed Stephen, "they were not able to withstand the wisdom and the Spirit by which he spake." Their jealousy and anger developed into deadly and murderous hate. They bribed men who reported that they had heard Stephen "speak blasphemous words against Moses, and against God." They stirred up against him the people as well as the rulers; they secured his arrest and then his arraignment before the chief council of the Jews. They set up false witnesses who accused him of speaking words against the Temple and the law, and of declaring that Jesus would destroy the Temple and change the religious rites established by Moses.

It is difficult from this narrative to understand exactly the nature of the charge against Stephen. Evidently it was partly true; his words, however, had been perverted, and a charge of this kind is always more difficult to meet. Upon reading the defense which follows, it is quite clear, however, that in testifying for Jesus, Stephen had predicted the destruction of Jerusalem, the passing away of Judaism, the universal character of Christianity, and the return of the Lord. These truths had been so interpreted and misstated as to ground the accusation of blasphemy. On such a charge Stephen was arraigned. Previously, only the Sadducees were bitter against the leaders of the church; but it is easy to see how the people and the Pharisees were now aroused, the former out of jealousy for the city and Temple to which they owed their livelihood, the latter because of their zeal for the law, the sanctity of which, they believed, had been attacked. Alone, yet fearless, Stephen stood to defend himself. Now, if ever, he was filled with the Holy Spirit; "and all that sat in the council, fastening their eyes on him, saw his face as it had been the face of an angel." The truest witnesses for Christ must expect opposition, hatred, and slander; but his Spirit will give them wisdom and strength in the hour of need, and will illumine their faces with a light which even their enemies will feel is not born of earth.

2. THE DEFENSE OF STEPHEN Ch. 7:1-53

1 And the high priest said, Are these things so? 2 And he said,

Brethren and fathers, hearken: The God of glory appeared unto our father Abraham, when he was in Mesopotamia, before he dwelt in Haran, 3 and said unto him, Get thee out of thy land, and from thy kindred, and come into the land which I shall show thee. 4 Then came he out of the land of the Chaldæans, and dwelt in Haran: and from thence, when his father was dead, God *removed him into this land, wherein ye now dwell: 5 and he gave him none inheritance in it, no, not so much as to set his foot on: and he promised that he would give it to him in posses- sion, and to his seed after him, when* as yet *he had no child. 6 And God spake on this wise, that his seed should sojourn in a strange land, and that they should bring them into bondage, and treat them ill, four hundred years. 7 And the nation to which they shall be in bondage will I judge, said God: and after that shall they come forth, and serve me in this place. 8 And he gave him the covenant of circumcision: and so* Abraham *begat Isaac, and circum- cised him the eighth day; and Isaac* begat *Jacob, and Jacob the twelve patriarchs. 9 And the patriarchs, moved with jealousy against Joseph, sold him into Egypt: and God was with him, 10 and delivered him out of all his afflictions, and gave him favor and wisdom before Pharaoh king of Egypt; and he made him governor over Egypt and all his house. 11 Now there came a famine over all Egypt and Canaan, and great affliction: and our fathers found no sus- tenance. 12 But when Jacob heard that there was grain in Egypt, he sent forth our fathers the first time. 13 And at the second time Joseph was made known to his brethren; and Joseph's race became manifest unto Pharaoh. 14 And Joseph sent, and called to him Jacob his father, and all his kindred, threescore and fifteen souls. 15 And Jacob went down into Egypt; and he died, himself and our fathers; 16 and they were carried over unto Shechem, and laid in the tomb that Abraham bought for a price in silver of the sons of Hamor in Shechem. 17 But as the time of the promise drew nigh which God vouchsafed unto Abraham, the people grew and multiplied in Egypt, 18 till there arose another king over Egypt, who knew not Joseph. 19 The same dealt craftily with our race, and ill-treated our fa- thers, that they should cast out their babes to the end they might not live. 20 At which season Moses was born, and was exceeding fair; and he was nourished three months in his father's house: 21 and when he was cast out, Pharaoh's daughter took him up, and nourished him for her own son. 22 And Moses was instructed in all the wisdom of the Egyptians; and he was mighty in his words and works.*

23 But when he was well-nigh forty years old, it came into his heart to visit his brethren the children of Israel. 24 And seeing one of them suffer wrong, he defended him, and avenged him that was oppressed, smiting the Egyptian: 25 and he supposed that his brethren understood that God by his hand was giving them deliverance; but they understood not. 26 And the day following he appeared unto them as they strove, and would have set them at one again, saying, Sirs, ye are brethren; why do ye wrong one to another? 27 But he that did his neighbor wrong thrust him away, saying, Who made thee a ruler and a judge over us? 28 Wouldest thou kill me, as thou killedst the Egyptian yesterday? 29 And Moses fled at this saying, and became a sojourner in the land of Midian, where he begat two sons. 30 And when forty years were fulfilled, an angel appeared to him in the wilderness of mount Sinai, in a flame of fire in a bush. 31 And when Moses saw it, he wondered at the sight: and as he drew near to behold, there came a voice of the Lord, 32 I am the God of thy fathers, the God of Abraham, and of Isaac, and of Jacob. And Moses trembled, and durst not behold. 33 And the Lord said unto him, Loose the shoes from thy feet: for the place whereon thou standest is holy ground. 34 I have surely seen the affliction of my people that is in Egypt, and have heard their groaning, and I am come down to deliver them: and now come, I will send thee into Egypt. 35 This Moses whom they refused, saying, Who made thee a ruler and a judge? him hath God sent to be both a ruler and a deliverer with the hand of the angel that appeared to him in the bush. 36 This man led them forth, having wrought wonders and signs in Egypt, and in the Red sea, and in the wilderness forty years. 37 This is that Moses, who said unto the children of Israel, A prophet shall God raise up unto you from among your brethren, like unto me. 38 This is he that was in the church in the wilderness with the angel that spake to him in the mount Sinai, and with our fathers: who received living oracles to give unto us: 39 to whom our fathers would not be obedient, but thrust him from them, and turned back in their hearts unto Egypt, 40 saying unto Aaron, Make us gods that shall go before us: for as for this Moses, who led us forth out of the land of

Egypt, we know not what is become of him. 41 And they made a calf in those days, and brought a sacrifice unto the idol, and rejoiced in the works of their hands. 42 But God turned, and gave them up to serve the host of heaven; as it is written in the book of the prophets,

> *Did ye offer unto me slain beasts and sacrifices*
> *Forty years in the wilderness, O house of Israel?*

43 And ye took up the tabernacle of Moloch,
> *And the star of the god Rephan,*
> *The figures which ye made to worship them:*
> *And I will carry you away beyond Babylon.*

44 Our fathers had the tabernacle of the testimony in the wilderness, even as he appointed who spake unto Moses, that he should make it according to the figure that he had seen. 45 Which also our fathers, in their turn, brought in with Joshua when they entered on the possession of the nations, that God thrust out before the face of our fathers, unto the days of David; 46 who found favor in the sight of God, and asked to find a habitation for the God of Jacob. 47 But Solomon built him a house. 48 Howbeit the Most High dwelleth not in houses made with hands; as saith the prophet,

49 The heaven is my throne,
> *And the earth the footstool of my feet:*
> *What manner of house will ye build me? saith the Lord:*
> *Or what is the place of my rest?*
50 Did not my hand make all these things?

51 Ye stiffnecked and uncircumcised in heart and ears, ye do always resist the Holy Spirit: as your fathers did, so do ye. 52 Which of the prophets did not your fathers persecute? and they killed them that showed before of the coming of the Righteous One; of whom ye have now become betrayers and murderers; 53 ye who received the law as it was ordained by angels, and kept it not.

The defense of Stephen was a historical argument vindicating him from the charge of blasphemy and convicting his judges of criminal unbelief. It was historical: therein first of all he showed his wisdom, for thereby alone could he for a time retain the interest and restrain the wrath of a hostile council of Jews; they would listen to the stories of their own patriarchs and heroes. It was also an argument; it was no random review or skillful epitome of Hebrew history, each statement and incident was a link in the chain of logic, and when the conclusion was stated it was held fast by every sentence which had previously been spoken. It vindicated Stephen and convicted the rulers, so that when its climax was reached there was little for them to do but either to kill their accuser or to confess their sin.

The argument worked out two parallel themes: (a) The revelation of God had always been progressive, and had never been confined to the Temple. (b) The messengers of God had always been rejected at first, but had been received later as divinely appointed deliverers. The first is summarized in the words: "The Most High dwelleth not in houses made with hands"; the second in the statement: "As your fathers did, so do ye." The first shows Stephen innocent of blasphemy; the second convicts his judges of opposing the will of God.

a. Stephen had been accused of blasphemy for declaring that God could be worshiped without the Temple and its rites; but, in referring to sacred history, he reminded his hearers in his first sentence that "the God of glory appeared unto . . . Abraham, when he was in Mesopotamia"—surely this was outside the Holy Land and the Temple. So he had revealed himself to Joseph in Egypt and to Moses in the wilderness. Even when the Temple was finally built, Solomon, in his prayer of dedication, had reminded the people that the Most High could not be confined to the precincts of any building. Step by step, the revelation of God had become more perfect, and it had reached its culmination in Christ, so Stephen seems to argue: first God revealed himself through a man, and then a family, and then a nation, and then a ceremonial, and finally in his Son. Toward the appearance of the Messiah all Jewish history had moved as to its goal; and now, through Christ, believers can worship God not only in the sacred mountain and the Temple, but wherever they turn to him "in spirit and truth." God has a message for each of us even when surrounded by pagans and unbelievers, as was Abraham in Mesopotamia; or when imprisoned and alone, as was Joseph in Egypt; or when driven into some wilderness by presumption and anger, as was Moses; or when worshiping by some ritual, as in the tabernacle; or when bowing beneath the beauties of some superb tabernacle, as did Solomon. However, all our experiences should be interpreted as designed to point us to Christ, and to lead us to find fellowship with God in him.

b. In his second argument, sustained by the same historic review, Stephen showed how unbelief has always been slow to accept the messages and messengers of God. Even Abraham tarried at Haran until his father was dead. Joseph was envied by his brothers and sold into Egypt, but later proved to be the savior of his family. Moses was driven into exile by his unbelieving nation, and even when he had brought them to Sinai, he was deserted by them; but in each instance, as he returned, he proved to be their deliverer. So Jesus had appeared, the divine Son of God; but, as Stephen argued, he had been envied by these Jewish rulers, and by them he had been rejected and crucified, but someday he would come again and be welcomed by a repentant people. Thus the rulers, in their blind attachment to Moses, whom Stephen was accused of blaspheming because he proclaimed Christ, were really opposing Moses, for he had predicted the coming of Christ; they claimed to be zealous for the law, but they were breaking the spirit of the law, and in their opposition to his Son they were really opposing and defying God. Thus one who today refuses allegiance to Christ is opposing God, and is excluding from his life the One who alone can bring brightness and joy. Someday this Christ will return and he who was mocked and crucified will be hailed as universal King and all the world will rejoice in the gladness of his reign.

3. THE DEATH OF STEPHEN   Chs. 7:54 to 8:3

54 Now when they heard these things, they were cut to the heart, and they gnashed on him with their teeth. 55 But he, being full of the Holy Spirit, looked up stedfastly into heaven, and saw the glory of God, and Jesus standing on the right hand of God, 56 and said, Behold, I see the heavens opened, and the Son of man standing on the right hand of God. 57 But they cried out with a loud voice, and stopped their ears, and rushed upon him with one accord; 58 and they cast him out of the city, and stoned him: and the witnesses laid down their garments at the feet of a young man named Saul. 59 And they stoned Stephen, calling upon the Lord, and saying, Lord Jesus, receive my spirit. 60 And he kneeled down, and cried with a loud voice, Lord, lay not this sin to their charge. And when he had said this, he fell asleep. 1 And Saul was consenting unto his death.

And there arose on that day a great persecution against the church which was in Jerusalem; and they were all scattered abroad throughout the regions of Judæa and Samaria, except the apostles. 2 And devout men buried Stephen, and made great lamentation over him. 3 But Saul laid waste the church, entering into every house, and dragging men and women committed them to prison.

In the defense of Stephen his two great arguments converged to a single point. Suddenly it burst upon his judges that every historic reference he had used indicated the divine mission of Jesus Christ, and emphasized their guilt and shame in rejecting and crucifying him. No wonder that "they were cut to the heart" and "gnashed on him with their teeth" and "cast him out of the city, and stoned him." It is evident that they did not pause for an official sentence, nor wait for the sanction of the Roman governor. They acted in blind rage and with heartless cruelty. The helpless victim, according to custom, was placed on a high rock, with hands tied behind him, and pushed forward that he might be killed by the fall; but as he still lived and knelt in prayer, they rushed upon him with stones and crushed him to death.

In this hour of peril and anguish, Stephen was full of the Holy Spirit and experienced what has been granted to other innocent sufferers who have testified boldly for Christ. First, there was a clearer vision of his Lord: He "saw the glory of God, and Jesus standing on the right hand of God." Such a vision beatific has been granted by the eye of faith to many heroes who have borne their bold testimony for Christ. Secondly, he was given a forgiving spirit. Like his Master he was enabled to pray: "Lord, lay not this sin to their charge." Only the power of Christ enables one so to pray. Thirdly, the peace of Christ ruled in his heart in that time of supreme agony. Amid that hail of stones and those shouts of hatred, "he fell asleep." For those who are faithful unto death a like divine peace has often been vouchsafed. Lastly, he received a "crown of life." His name means "crown" and we are sure that this awaited him, as it awaits all who are true to their Lord and look for his appearing. Yet there was a reward of priceless value in the influence which came from the witness of this first martyr. There was present as a witness "a young man named Saul." It is probably true that "if Stephen had not so prayed, Paul had not preached," and it is beyond question that the brightest crown that falls to those who suffer for the name of Christ consists in the imperishable influence which falls upon those who witness their heroism and courage.

The death of Stephen had, however, an immediate and startling consequence. By it were lighted the fires of a fierce persecution. Of this Saul was the leader. It resulted in the scattering abroad of the Christians "throughout the regions of Judæa and Samaria." It involved pain, sorrow, separation, sufferings, loss; yet it issued in a wider preaching of the gospel. Until now the church had made no effort to testify for Christ outside the city of Jerusalem; the persecution which arose in connection with the death of Stephen was the occasion of a movement which was to carry the good news of salvation "unto the uttermost part of the earth."

II
THE BROADENING
OF THE CHURCH

THE WITNESS IN SAMARIA
AND JUDEA
Chs. 8:4 to 12:25

A. THE PREACHING OF PHILIP Ch. 8:4-40

1. THE GOSPEL IN SAMARIA   Ch. 8:4-25

4 They therefore that were scattered abroad went about preaching the word. 5 And Philip went down to the city of Samaria, and proclaimed unto them the Christ. 6 And the multitudes gave heed with one accord unto the things that were spoken by Philip, when they heard, and saw the signs which he did. 7 For from many of those that had unclean spirits, they came out, crying with a loud voice: and many that were palsied, and that were lame, were healed. 8 And there was much joy in that city.

9 But there was a certain man, Simon by name, who beforetime in the city used sorcery, and amazed the people of Samaria, giving out that himself was some great one: 10 to whom they all gave heed, from the least to the greatest, saying, This man is that power of God which is called Great. 11 And they gave heed to him, because that of long time he had amazed them with his sorceries. 12 But when they believed Philip preaching good tidings concerning the kingdom of God and the name of Jesus Christ, they were baptized, both men and women. 13 And Simon also himself believed: and being baptized, he continued with Philip; and beholding signs and great miracles wrought, he was amazed.

14 Now when the apostles that were at Jerusalem heard

that Samaria had received the word of God, they sent unto them Peter and John: 15 who, when they were come down, prayed for them, that they might receive the Holy Spirit: 16 for as yet it was fallen upon none of them: only they had been baptized into the name of the Lord Jesus. 17 Then laid they their hands on them, and they received the Holy Spirit. 18 Now when Simon saw that through the laying on of the apostles' hands the Holy Spirit was given, he offered them money, 19 saying, Give me also this power, that on whomsoever I lay my hands, he may receive the Holy Spirit. 20 But Peter said unto him, Thy silver perish with thee, because thou hast thought to obtain the gift of God with money. 21 Thou hast neither part nor lot in this matter: for thy heart is not right before God. 22 Repent therefore of this thy wickedness, and pray the Lord, if perhaps the thought of thy heart shall be forgiven thee. 23 For I see that thou art in the gall of bitterness and in the bond of iniquity. 24 And Simon answered and said, Pray ye for me to the Lord, that none of the things which ye have spoken come upon me.

25 They therefore, when they had testified and spoken the word of the Lord, returned to Jerusalem, and preached the gospel to many villages of the Samaritans.

The preaching of Philip opens what may be regarded as a distinct section in the story of The Acts. The first seven chapters show how the church was founded; but its witness for Christ was confined to the city of Jerusalem, and the converts were all of Jewish birth. These five chapters, the eighth to the twelfth inclusive, tell how the good news was carried to Judea and Samaria and even as far north as Antioch, and how Gentiles were admitted to membership in the church. It describes a period of transition: the horizon of the church is broadening, and preparation is being made for the great missionary journeys of Paul which fill the remaining chapters of the book. The interesting material of this intermediate section is grouped around the names of Philip, Saul, Peter, Cornelius, Barnabas, and Herod.

This Philip was not the apostle of that name, but one of the seven "deacons," who was subsequently known as "the evangelist." That title appears in connection with no other New Testament name. He was, of course, not the only evangelist; yet his work was so distinctive that a study of his career reveals the great principles relative to evangelistic preaching and methods, and emphasizes particularly the power of the Spirit upon whom success in such work ultimately depends.

In a real sense all believers became evangelists; for we read that "they were all scattered abroad . . . , except the apostles," and "they therefore that were scattered abroad went about preaching the word." The "therefore" is full of significance. It was because of the fierce persecution that had burst upon the church, because of banishment and exile and homelessness and weary wanderings, that these early Christians carried "the good news" beyond the confines of Jerusalem. Thus God often overrules evil for good; thus, in hours of shadow, Christians have often seen the path of duty more clearly. At such great cost, too, the gospel message has ever been carried to "the regions beyond."

Among these fugitives from Jerusalem many may have been equally faithful, but none became as famous as Philip. He fled to Samaria, probably to its capital city, and there with such power proclaimed the faith for which he had been persecuted that the resulting events have been called "the Samaritan Pentecost." As on that first great day of ingathering, multitudes listened to the witness concerning Christ; the truth of the message was attested likewise by marvelous miracles; great numbers were converted, and "there was much joy in that city," as indeed there is in every city where the gospel is faithfully proclaimed.

The significant fact is that a Jew was preaching to Samaritans, and Samaritans were rejoicing in the message of a Jew; for Jews were supposed to have no dealings with Samaritans, and until now Jewish converts to Christianity had preached only to men of their own race. Even this, however, was less startling than the conversion of Gentiles would be. Samaritans were despised, yet they were only half heathen and their religion was really a debased Judaism. This was a great step in the broadening of the church, yet it was the easiest possible step; it was a natural transition to the position that Gentiles and Jews form one body in Christ. Race prejudices still exist, and even some Christians take a provincial view of the mission of the church. It is necessary today to enforce the lessons of this chapter and of the chapters which immediately follow.

It is also significant that the man who became known as "the evangelist" was a "layman," as many of his greatest successors have been. The example is a summons, not to disregard ordination, for Philip was ordained as an officer in the church and this in view of his mental and spiritual attainments, but a summons to employ every natural ability and every providential opportunity to witness faithfully for Christ.

It is further to be noted that "the evangelist" labored where the gospel had not been proclaimed; his work was that of a modern missionary, and the term "evangelist" is used most exactly where it describes one who labors among those to whom the good news of salvation has not otherwise been brought.

The great success of the work accomplished by Philip in Samaria is attested by two striking incidents: the first is the experience of Simon, the sorcerer, the second is the new gift of the Holy Spirit.

In the traditions of the early centuries this Simon Magus occupies a large place as a reputed enemy of the church. So far as the story of The Acts is concerned, he appears as a clever and unscrupulous magician, who by his arts and deceptions has played upon the ignorance and credulity of his followers so that they might accept his crude and mystical teachings, and more particularly might enrich him by their gifts. He had so impressed the people of Samaria that they regarded him as an incarnation of divine power, calling him "that power of God which is called Great." The success of Philip is evidenced, then, by the fact that all the people turned to him from Simon, and that even "Simon also himself believed: and being baptized, he continued with Philip." Of course, his belief was quite imperfect; the sequel shows that he experienced neither true repentance nor faith. His influence over the people, however, was destroyed, and he was himself convinced that in the name of Jesus there was a power he himself had never known. He is thus the symbol of the false religious teachers, past and present, mystical, deceiving, selfish, who have opposed the gospel, but have been overcome by its power.

The gift of the Holy Spirit to the Samaritan converts was granted through the agency of the apostles, Peter and John, who were sent from Jerusalem to investigate the work of Philip. This gift does not here denote the usual influence of the Spirit which results in repentance and faith and holiness, but the extraordinary and miraculous "gifts" which were frequently bestowed upon believers, particularly in the early days of the apostolic church. These signs had the specific design of attesting the truth, and as here in Samaria, they were evidences of the new life which resulted from faith in Christ. Even the apostles had no power to confer these gifts; but the fact that they prayed for their bestowal shows that the apostles recognized the fact that Samaritans had actually become Christians, and that the apostles gave their sanction to the new step which Philip had taken in preaching the gospel to those who were not Jews.

This mission of Peter and John, their prayer, and the miraculous gifts, also demonstrated the unity of the church. It suggested that there were real converts in Samaria, but also that they belonged to the same body as the believers in Jerusalem, and should recognize the leadership and official position of the apostles. Thus in all evangelistic work those who profess conversion should be examined by church officers and should be brought into the organized life of the church.

The interval of time which here elapsed between the acceptance of Christ and the gift of the Holy Spirit is not intended to teach that spiritual life or gifts or graces come from "the laying on of the apostles' hands," nor yet does it support the theory that there is always an interval between conversion and the "fulness of the Spirit," or the "baptism of the Spirit," nor that converts must seek a "second blessing." In the typical case of Cornelius and his friends the gift came without laying on of hands and before any interval of time had elapsed. This experience of the Samaritans was exceptional and was intended to teach further that, as miraculous gifts might be withheld for a time from true converts, so in the future, as at the present day, conversion might be quite as real even though attended by no miracles or signs.

The effect of this incident upon Simon Magus and his interview with Peter reveal the actual state of his heart, and emphasize his complete discomfiture and defeat. He offered to purchase from the apostles the power to confer these supernatural gifts of the Holy Spirit, thus suggesting that it was his intention to sell the same. All traffic in things sacred has been called "simony" from the name of this ancient sorcerer; and all who are tempted to make gain from holy offices or spiritual gifts do well to ponder the solemn, searching rebuke which fell from the lips of Peter. The words of Peter, however, are not to be regarded as an imprecation or a curse. They contain a call to repentance, but intimate that there is small hope that Simon will or can change his evil course. His reply to Peter expresses fear but no real contrition; it indicates, however, how completely Simon, the popular leader, has been discredited and silenced.

The story closes with the statement that as they journey to Jerusalem, the apostles turn evangelists and, while themselves Jews, proclaim the gospel "to many villages of the Samaritans." Thus their horizon is broadening and soon they will rejoice that to the Gentiles also the good news is being preached.

2. THE CONVERSION OF AN ETHIOPIAN
Ch. 8:26-40

26 But an angel of the Lord spake unto Philip, saying, Arise, and go toward the south unto the way that goeth down from Jerusalem unto Gaza: the same is desert. 27 And he arose and went: and behold, a man of Ethiopia, a eunuch of great authority under Candace, queen of the Ethiopians, who was over all her treasure, who had come to Jerusalem to worship; 28 and he was returning and sitting in his chariot, and was reading the prophet Isaiah. 29 And the Spirit said unto Philip, Go near, and join thyself to this chariot. 30 And Philip ran to him, and heard him reading Isaiah the prophet, and said, Understandest thou what thou readest? 31 And he said, How can I, except some one shall guide me? And he besought Philip to come up and sit with him. 32 Now the passage of the scripture which he was reading was this,

He was led as a sheep to the slaughter;
And as a lamb before his shearer is dumb,
So he openeth not his mouth:
33 In his humiliation his judgment was taken away:
His generation who shall declare?
For his life is taken from the earth.
34 And the eunuch answered Philip, and said, I pray thee, of whom speaketh the prophet this? of himself, or of some other? 35 And Philip opened his mouth, and beginning from this scripture, preached unto him Jesus. 36 And as they went on the way, they came unto a certain water; and the eunuch saith, Behold, here is water; what doth hinder me to be baptized? 38 And he commanded the chariot to stand still: and they both went down into the water, both Philip and the eunuch; and he baptized him. 39 And when they came up out of the water, the Spirit of the Lord caught away Philip; and the eunuch saw him no more, for

*he went on his way rejoicing. 40 But Philip was found at
Azotus: and passing through he preached the gospel to all
the cities, till he came to Cæsarea.*

From his great work in the city of Samaria, Philip was
suddenly summoned to the desert hills of southern Judea.
Instead of addressing multitudes he was to bring the gospel message to one man; but the task is no less difficult
and, to the mind of the Master, it is no less important.
The man who preaches Christ to eager crowds is no more
truly an evangelist than he who testifies for his Lord to a
chance acquaintance on a lonely journey. The comparative results are known only to God. The man whom
Philip found on the road which led down from Jerusalem
to Gaza was none other than the chancellor of the ex-
chequer of Candace, queen of the Ethiopians. He became
a Christian missionary to the continent of Africa. Philip
and the apostles, having learned that the gospel was to be
preached in Samaria as well as in Jerusalem, were reminded again that they were to be witnesses "unto the uttermost part of the earth."

For another reason the conversion of this Ethiopian
ruler is congruous to the period through which the church
was passing; it was a time of transition, and the horizon
was broadening gradually; Philip might have hesitated to
offer Christ to a pagan; but this man, not a Jew by birth,
was surely no "heathen"; he had been to Jerusalem "to
worship"; he was reading the Old Testament. He was
exactly the man to make easy the step which changed the
Christians from missionaries among the Jews to witnesses
in all the wide world.

Possibly the most practical lessons which lie on the surface of this fascinating narrative are those which guide and
encourage such as are willing, in private, personal conver-
sation, to "do the work of an evangelist":

a. Opportunities are found in most unexpected places.
To one who was accustomed to the throngs in Samaria, the

desert road to Gaza must have seemed to promise a poor field of labor; but there it was that Philip met the Ethiopian prince. To those who are willing to follow divine guidance, surprising openings for testimony are certain to appear.

b. These opportunities are fleeting. The Spirit said, "Go," and "Philip ran." This is picturesque and instructive. Had the chariot rolled by, as far as the evangelist was concerned, it would have been gone forever. Work for Christ demands immediate obedience to every prompting of his Spirit.

c. The way is prepared for all who obey the voice of the Spirit. When Philip drew near to the chariot the eunuch was reading "the prophet Isaiah," and he had opened the book at the fifty-third chapter; how could he have been made ready more perfectly for the message the evangelist was to bring? One who is sent by the Lord to speak to a needy soul will find that the Master has gone before him to prepare the heart of the hearer.

d. In addition to the Bible there is needed a human teacher if the way of salvation is to be made plain. There are exceptional cases, but the rule is expressed by the Ethiopian prince. He had the written word, but when Philip asked whether he understood he replied: "How can I, except some one shall guide me?"

e. The message of Philip embodied the heart of the gospel; it declared that Jesus of Nazareth was the suffering Savior, the Lamb of God who came to take away the sin of the world. This is the burden of the "good news" proclaimed by every true evangelist.

f. The words of Philip evidently included instruction relative to the rite of Christian baptism. Evangelism must aim to secure an open profession of faith on the part of everyone who accepts Christ.

g. Philip was suddenly "caught away" from the rejoicing convert, and passed on to Caesarea which became his home. When next he appears in the story he is pictured as the host who is entertaining missionaries and training his daughters to testify for Christ; at this time he is called "the evangelist." This suggests a third form of evangelistic service. One may be called to preach to thousands as was Philip in Samaria, or to speak to one man as in the desert of Judea; but he may be evangelizing the world quite as truly by the aid he gives to religious workers, and by exerting the abiding influence of a Christian home.

B. THE CONVERSION OF SAUL Ch. 9:1-30

1 But Saul, yet breathing threatening and slaughter against the disciples of the Lord, went unto the high priest, 2 and asked of him letters to Damascus unto the synagogues, that if he found any that were of the Way, whether men or women, he might bring them bound to Jerusalem. 3 And as he journeyed, it came to pass that he drew nigh unto Damascus: and suddenly there shone round about him a light out of heaven: 4 and he fell upon the earth, and heard a voice saying unto him, Saul, Saul, why persecutest thou me? 5 And he said, Who art thou, Lord? And he said, *I am Jesus whom thou persecutest: 6 but rise, and enter into the city, and it shall be told thee what thou must do. 7 And the men that journeyed with him stood speechless, hearing the voice, but beholding no man. 8 And Saul arose from the earth; and when his eyes were opened, he saw nothing; and they led him by the hand, and brought him into Damascus. 9 And he was three days without sight, and did neither eat nor drink.*

10 Now there was a certain disciple at Damascus, named Ananias; and the Lord said unto him in a vision, Ananias. And he said, Behold, I am here, Lord. 11 And the Lord said unto him, Arise, and go to the street which is called Straight, and inquire in the house of Judas for one named Saul, a man of Tarsus: for behold, he prayeth; 12 and he hath seen a man named Ananias coming in, and laying his hands on him, that he might receive his sight. 13 But Ananias answered, Lord, I have heard from many of this man, how much evil he did to thy saints at Jeru-

salem: 14 and here he hath authority from the chief
priests to bind all that call upon thy name. 15 But the
Lord said unto him, Go thy way: for he is a chosen vessel
unto me, to bear my name before the Gentiles and kings,
and the children of Israel: 16 for I will show him how
many things he must suffer for my name's sake. 17 And
Ananias departed, and entered into the house; and laying
his hands on him said, Brother Saul, the Lord, even Jesus,
who appeared unto thee in the way which thou camest,
hath sent me, that thou mayest receive thy sight, and be
filled with the Holy Spirit. 18 And straightway there fell
from his eyes as it were scales, and he received his sight;
and he arose and was baptized; 19 and he took food and
was strengthened.

And he was certain days with the disciples that were at
Damascus. 20 And straightway in the synagogues he proclaimed Jesus, that he is the Son of God. 21 And all that
heard him were amazed, and said, Is not this he that in
Jerusalem made havoc of them that called on this name?
and he had come hither for this intent, that he might bring
them bound before the chief priests. 22 But Saul increased the more in strength, and confounded the Jews that
dwelt at Damascus, proving that this is the Christ.

23 And when many days were fulfilled, the Jews took
counsel together to kill him: 24 but their plot became
known to Saul. And they watched the gates also day and
night that they might kill him: 25 but his disciples took
him by night, and let him down through the wall, lowering
him in a basket.

26 And when he was come to Jerusalem, he assayed to
join himself to the disciples: and they were all afraid of
him, not believing that he was a disciple. 27 But Barnabas
took him, and brought him to the apostles, and declared
unto them how he had seen the Lord in the way, and that
he had spoken to him, and how at Damascus he had
preached boldly in the name of Jesus. 28 And he was
with them going in and going out at Jerusalem, 29 preaching boldly in the name of the Lord: and he spake and disputed against the Grecian Jews; but they were seeking to
kill him. 30 And when the brethren knew it, they brought
him down to Cæsarea, and sent him forth to Tarsus.

The conversion of Saul of Tarsus, who is better known as Paul the apostle, was an event of supreme importance in the history of the church and thus of the world. This might be concluded from the prominent place given to its record in the story of The Acts; three times it is repeated: first, as written by Luke for his Christian readers; second, as told by Paul to a mob of Jews; and third, as rehearsed by the apostle in the presence of the Roman rulers.

The narrative is of deep significance in the present day. First, it affords on of the strongest evidences of the truth of the Christian faith; for how can one account for the career of Paul if he was not thus converted, and how account for his conversion if Jesus the crucified is not the divine and risen Christ? Secondly, the story is full of encouragement to all who witness for Christ; for Paul was brought into Christian life and service by the testimony of an obscure disciple named Ananias, and the suggestion is evident that faithful effort may result in the conversion of one whose career may influence generations and races of men. Thirdly, the immediate public confession of Christ on the part of Saul is an example which should give to fainthearted, secret believers courage to act in accordance with their convictions.

The historian Luke inevitably places this story in the section of The Acts which describes the preparation of the church for its worldwide witness, for here he shows how a new apostle was chosen and appointed as the principal messenger to the Gentile world. Saul had been providentially prepared for his task; by birth a Jew, but also possessing Roman citizenship, spending his early years under the influence of Greek culture in the university city of Tarsus, and later trained in the knowledge of the sacred Scriptures as a student in Jerusalem, his experiences adapted him to appreciate all the elements and phases of thought and belief which entered into the life of the world in the age to which he belonged.

Then again his character qualified him for his eminent

service; he was a man of strong intellect, yet of tender emotions, and possessing a genius for religion; this unusual combination produced a personality at once interesting, compelling, and forceful. At the time of his conversion he was in the full maturity of his powers, favorably known in Jerusalem, and occupying a position of wide influence. The event is immediately connected with the death of Stephen and the persecution which then arose. As narrated by the historian attention is fixed: (1) upon Saul's conviction of sin, (2) upon his acceptance of Christ, and (3) upon his confession of faith.

1. It was a vision of the risen and glorified Christ which wrought in the soul of Saul a deep conviction of sin. He had been a striking example of the truth that a man may be sincere and moral, even intensely religious, and yet be stained with guilt. His outward life had been blameless; so zealous was he of the faith of his fathers, and so certain that he was doing God service, that with no qualm of conscience he arrested, tortured, and caused to blaspheme, all who had accepted the new faith; he gave his vote as a ruler to have them put to death. So fanatical was his zeal that he pursued them even to foreign cities. On such a quest, armed with letters from the high priest, he was drawing near to the city of Damascus, when suddenly there burst upon him a light surpassing the brightness of the Syrian sun at noonday, and he heard the voice of the Lord saying to him, "Saul, Saul, why persecutest thou me?" And Saul said, "Who art thou, Lord?" And the Lord said, "I am Jesus whom thou persecutest." Paul actually saw Christ. His experience was no mere mental impression, no hallucination, no feverish fancy induced by sunstroke. He always insisted that he at that time as truly looked upon the risen Lord as did the disciples in the upper room on the evening of that first "Easter." He claimed to be literally a witness of the resurrection and on this fact he based his apostolic authority.

The words which accompanied the vision assured Paul

that Christ so identified himself with his followers that one who persecuted them was guilty of offering violence to the Lord of glory. How futile and mad such a course must be was enforced by the words recorded in a later version of the story: "It is hard for thee to kick against the goad." To attempt to oppose Christ, to endeavor to destroy his church, was as certain to result in injury to the persecutor, as the attempt of an infuriated ox to kick against the iron-shod goad of the driver. In an instant Saul appreciated the whole truth; Jesus was the divine Son of God; in persecuting his followers he had been guilty of an incomparable crime; he was himself the chief of sinners. In penitence and sorrow and shame and submission he cries out, "What shall I do, Lord?" He rises from the ground to which he has fallen, blind and helpless, and in spiritual bewilderment and darkness; but there has come to him a word of promise: "Enter into the city, and it shall be told thee what thou must do." Thus led by the hand the once proud persecutor enters Damascus and continues three days without food or sight; but new light and life are sure to come, for he has submitted his will to the will of the Lord.

Thus it is ever; a new vision of Christ in his divine holiness and power and mercy must result in a consciousness of sin; but the darkest night of penitence is sure to issue in the dawn of a larger and more glorious life.

2. The acceptance of Christ as a personal Savior was due, in the case of Saul, to the guidance of an obscure Jewish convert in Damascus named Ananias. When he was summoned to this task which was to result in a blessing to the whole world, Ananias at first hesitated to go; he feared to approach the cruel persecutor who had come to the city for the express purpose of arresting all who professed to follow Christ. His reluctance was overcome by the divine assurance of the great work which Paul was destined to achieve. This consideration of the possible issue of their testimony has overcome the fears of count-

less Christian messengers when facing difficult tasks in all ages.

As is usual in such cases, the messenger found the way prepared before him. Saul was in prayer and moreover, was expecting the coming of Ananias, who explained to his eager listener the gospel of grace, the forgiveness of sins, the necessity of baptism, and the gift of the Holy Spirit. Then as Saul accepted the truth his eyes were opened and at the same time the blindness of his soul was removed, his sins were washed away, and at the touch of Ananias he was filled with the Holy Spirit. It is noticeable that the latter gift was imparted at the hands of a layman; the selection of Saul, and his appointment to service, were thus quite independent of the twelve apostles. A new apostle was thus chosen in a Gentile city to be the supreme witness for Christ unto the uttermost part of the Gentile world.

3. The confession of faith was immediate and heroic. The story should be pondered by all who hesitate to acknowledge their secret allegiance to Christ. Of course it occasioned surprise to the whole city of Damascus; but should one fear what men may think or say, if he knows he is obeying the will of his Lord? It involved danger and suffering; for a plot was formed against his life, and Saul was compelled to flee under cover of night; but none need expect to enter the Kingdom of Heaven without persecution and opposition. It exposed Saul to suspicion and misunderstanding; this is a common experience for those who confess their Christian faith; in fact, many persons hesitate to make such confession for fear of being regarded as hypocrites. Even the disciples in Jerusalem regarded Saul as an impostor and a spy; yet it is better to have the world regard us as false when we know we are sincere, than to have the world trust us when in our hearts we know we are untrue to the Christ we are afraid to confess; a secret believer is a hypocrite.

Confession resulted, however, in unequaled usefulness.

Driven from Jerusalem as he had been from Damascus, Saul returned to the city of his birth. One's home is always the first and best place for Christian testimony. A little later he was called to assist Barnabas in Antioch and thence he passed on to a career of testimony which has changed the currents of human history. Today the world is waiting for the blessed influence of such men, who have the courage of their convictions, and who in all the relations of life will be openly loyal to their divine Master.

C. THE JOURNEYS OF PETER Ch. 9:31-43

31 So the church throughout all Judæa and Galilee and Samaria had peace, being edified; and, walking in the fear of the Lord and in the comfort of the Holy Spirit, was multiplied.

32 And it came to pass, as Peter went throughout all parts, he came down also to the saints that dwelt at Lydda. 33 And there he found a certain man named Æneas, who had kept his bed eight years; for he was palsied. 34 And Peter said unto him, Æneas, Jesus Christ healeth thee: arise, and make thy bed. And straightway he arose. 35 And all that dwelt at Lydda and in Sharon saw him, and they turned to the Lord.

36 Now there was at Joppa a certain disciple named Tabitha, which by interpretation is called Dorcas: this woman was full of good works and almsdeeds which she did. 37 And it came to pass in those days, that she fell sick, and died: and when they had washed her, they laid her in an upper chamber. 38 And as Lydda was nigh unto Joppa, the disciples, hearing that Peter was there, sent two men unto him, entreating him, Delay not to come on unto us. 39 And Peter arose and went with them. And when he was come, they brought him into the upper chamber: and all the widows stood by him weeping, and showing the coats and garments which Dorcas made, while she was with them. 40 But Peter put them all forth, and kneeled down, and prayed; and turning to the body, he said, Tabitha, arise. And she opened her eyes; and when she saw Peter, she sat up. 41 And he gave her his hand, and raised her

*up; and calling the saints and widows, he presented her
alive. 42 And it became known throughout all Joppa: and
many believed on the Lord. 43 And it came to pass, that
he abode many days in Joppa with one Simon a tanner.*

The conversion of Saul, the leading persecutor, was followed by a season of rest and growth for the Christian
church. Since the death of Stephen the history has been
concerned chiefly with the work of Philip and the mission
of Ananias, both laymen. That does not mean, however,
that the apostles were inactive. Their ministry has been
passed in almost complete silence, because the church was
being prepared by other agents for its wider testimony; but
now the journeys of Peter are recorded, for they brought
him to Joppa, within call of Caesarea, in which city he
was to perform the supreme work of this period of transition. He was to open the door of the church for the reception of Gentile believers.

Nevertheless, Peter's progress through Judea was in itself important; he strengthened the church, he secured new
converts, and he worked two notable miracles. The healing of Aeneas, who was sick of the palsy, recalls some of
the most memorable scenes in the life of Christ, by whose
power this sufferer was now relieved from the anguish of
eight long years of painful illness. The cure was so marvelous that it resulted in the conversion of a multitude in
Lydda and Sharon.

Of Dorcas, or Tabitha, nothing is known except this
one startling story. Death had overtaken her in the midst
of a life of blessed ministry and helpfulness. Her friends,
in distress, but evidently in faith, summoned Peter to
Joppa; and in answer to his prayer the sleeping saint
awoke. This raising to life of one who had been dead was
the most marvelous miracle the apostles had performed.
No wonder that it wrought faith in many hearts, and that
as its result "many believed on the Lord." As to Dorcas,
it may be remarked that her Christian charity has set in

motion innumerable needles and has inspired countless
women with the spirit of service. As to Peter, he was
about to be summoned to a task more astonishing to the
early church than the healing of Aeneas or the raising of
Dorcas from the dead.

D. THE RECEPTION OF CORNELIUS
Chs. 10:1 to 11:18

Possibly Cornelius was not the first Gentile convert,
but he was the first Gentile whose conversion is recorded.
The Cyprian and Cyrenian missionaries may have
preached previously to Greeks in Antioch (Acts 11:19-
20), but the case of Cornelius was in many points unique
and of such surpassing importance that it is narrated with
repetitious and minute details. Here an apostle, under divine guidance, goes to preach to a Roman officer, and here
Gentiles are formally welcomed into the church. Here
the legitimacy of Gentile Christianity is recognized and
established. Furthermore, the instance is typical, so that
all who would study the facts of conversion, and the truth
concerning the Holy Spirit in his relation to believers, must
ponder this inspired narrative. It is one of the turning
points in Christian history, and an outstanding feature in
the period when the church was being prepared for its
worldwide witness.

At first only Jews were evangelized, then Samaritans
also, but now a representative Gentile and a large circle
of his friends are led to accept Christ and are filled with his
Spirit, so that this incident has been known as the "Roman
Pentecost."

1. THE MAN   Ch. 10:1-8

1 Now there was *a certain man in Cæsarea, Cornelius
by name, a centurion of the band called the Italian* band,
*2 a devout man, and one that feared God with all his
house, who gave much alms to the people, and prayed to*

God always. 3 He saw in a vision openly, as it were about the ninth hour of the day, an angel of God coming in unto him, and saying to him, Cornelius. 4 And he, fastening his eyes upon him, and being affrighted, said, What is it, Lord? And he said unto him, Thy prayers and thine alms are gone up for a memorial before God. 5 And now send men to Joppa, and fetch one Simon, who is surnamed Peter: 6 he lodgeth with one Simon a tanner, whose house is by the sea side. 7 And when the angel that spake unto him was departed, he called two of his household-servants, and a devout soldier of them that waited on him continually; 8 and having rehearsed all things unto them, he sent them to Joppa.

Cornelius the centurion was in command of a military company known as the "Italian band," or cohort. He was stationed at Caesarea, the capital city of the Roman province. Like the three other centurions mentioned in the New Testament he was a man of high character. His name indicates that he was of illustrious, if not noble, birth. He had come to know and worship the one true God, and his sincere piety had inspired a like faith in all his household. His generosity was attested by liberal gifts to his Jewish neighbors whom other Romans despised and abused. He was a man of prayer, and in the midst of his busy life he observed the regular periods prescribed by the Jews at nine and twelve and three o'clock daily. Yet this noble, godly, generous, prayerful man was not saved; for as he was praying an angel appeared to him and bade him send to Joppa for Peter, who would tell him words whereby he and his family might be saved. (Ch. 11:13-14.)

It is almost startling to note the character of the men who are described in The Acts as needing the salvation that can be found in Christ alone. This section of the book narrates three notable conversions: that of the Ethiopian prince, of Saul, and of Cornelius, but all of these were godly men; they were not only of irreproachable morality but they were zealously religious. Are such men lost? Is it absolutely necessary today for men of this character to experience a "new birth"? These narratives seem so to affirm, and they remind us of the words spoken by our Lord to the great teacher of Israel: "Ye must be born anew."

It should be added at once, however, that to men of this character, who are living according to the light they have, more light is sure to be given; and then, too, when the new light comes, it is sure to be accepted. When Christ is presented to men like these, they turn to him at once in penitence and faith. Thus sincerity is tested. Christ is ever the touchstone of character.

The source of new light was revealed to Cornelius by an angel, and his sincerity was attested by the speed with which he sent to summon the appointed messenger. The angel visitant emphasized the importance of the event which was to follow, namely, the formal opening of the church to Gentile believers; but the fact that the angel did not tell the way of salvation, but commanded Cornelius to send for Peter, calls to mind the important truth that the gospel message, on which salvation depends, is to be proclaimed, not by supernatural messengers, but by men to their fellowmen.

2. THE MESSENGER   Ch. 10:9-23

9 Now on the morrow, as they were on their journey, and drew nigh unto the city, Peter went up upon the housetop to pray, about the sixth hour: 10 and he became hungry, and desired to eat: but while they made ready, he fell into a trance; 11 and he beholdeth the heaven opened, and a certain vessel descending, as it were a great sheet, let down by four corners upon the earth: 12 wherein were all manner of fourfooted beasts and creeping things of the earth and birds of the heaven. 13 And there came a voice to him, Rise, Peter; kill and eat. 14 But Peter said, Not so, Lord; for I have never eaten anything that is common and unclean.   15 And a voice came unto him again the second time, What God hath cleansed, make not thou common.   16 And this was done thrice: and straightway the vessel was received up into heaven.

17 Now while Peter was much perplexed in himself what the vision which he had seen might mean, behold, the men that were sent by Cornelius, having made inquiry for Simon's house, stood before the gate, 18 and called and asked whether Simon, who was surnamed Peter, were lodging there.   19 And while Peter thought on the vision, the Spirit said unto him, Behold, three men seek thee.   20 But arise, and get thee down, and go with them, nothing doubting: for I have sent them.   21 And Peter went down to the men, and said, Behold, I am he whom ye seek: what is the cause wherefore ye are come?   22 And they said, Cornelius a centurion, a righteous man and one that feareth God, and well reported of by all the nation of the Jews, was warned of God by a holy angel to send for thee into his house, and to hear words from thee.   23 So he called them in and lodged them.

And on the morrow he arose and went forth with them, and certain of the brethren from Joppa accompanied him.

By a series of providences Peter, the chosen messenger, had been brought within calling distance, but he was now to receive a special preparation for his task.   He needed to have his prejudices removed before he could be willing to undertake his work.   Peter might have consented to preach to Gentiles, but he would have refused to eat with them or to accept believing Gentiles into the Christian brotherhood.   The gulf between Jew and Gentile was greater than can be imagined today.   To the former the Gentile was an abomination; his touch defiled, his customs were abhorrent, his religion was a blasphemy. Therefore a vision was given to Peter to teach him that those whom God might cleanse should not be regarded as unclean.

While praying upon the flat housetop of Simon the tan-

ner in Joppa, as the noon hour is passing, Peter becomes
hungry and increasingly so as dinner is delayed. He falls
into a trance and beholds a vessel let down from heaven
full of animals, some ceremonially clean and fit for food,
others, to a Jew, unclean and not to be eaten. The clean
have been made unclean by contact with the unclean—
that is the point. Three times the vessel appears; each
time Peter is bidden by a heavenly voice to eat; each time
he refuses; each time he is rebuked by the words: "What
God hath cleansed, make not thou common." Just then
the messengers arrive and invite him to the home of Cornelius the Gentile. Before the vision, Peter would have refused; now the invitation explains the vision and he is willing to go. He has learned that at the command of God he
is not to shrink from contact with men of other nations,
nor fear to accept them as brothers in case God has
cleansed their hearts. The first paragraph of the story tells
us that even godly men like Cornelius need the gospel; this
paragraph assures us that even the most despised can be
transformed by its power. The first great qualifications
needed by Christian witnesses are a willingness to speak to
anyone to whom they may be sent, and a sympathy so
broad as to welcome as brothers believers of every race
and nation.

3. THE MEETING   Ch. 10:24-33

*24 And on the morrow they entered into Cæsarea. And
Cornelius was waiting for them, having called together his
kinsmen and his near friends. 25 And when it came to
pass that Peter entered, Cornelius met him, and fell down
at his feet, and worshipped him. 26 But Peter raised him
up, saying, Stand up; I myself also am a man. 27 And as
he talked with him, he went in, and findeth many come together: 28 and he said unto them, Ye yourselves know
how it is an unlawful thing for a man that is a Jew to join
himself or come unto one of another nation; and yet unto
me hath God showed that I should not call any man common or unclean: 29 wherefore also I came without gain-*

*saying, when I was sent for. I ask therefore with what in-
tent ye sent for me. 30 And Cornelius said, Four days
ago, until this hour, I was keeping the ninth hour of prayer
in my house; and behold, a man stood before me in bright
apparel, 31 and saith, Cornelius, thy prayer is heard, and
thine alms are had in remembrance in the sight of God.
32 Send therefore to Joppa, and call unto thee Simon,
who is surnamed Peter; he lodgeth in the house of Simon
a tanner, by the sea side. 33 Forthwith therefore I sent
to thee; and thou hast well done that thou art come. Now
therefore we are all here present in the sight of God, to
hear all things that have been commanded thee of the
Lord.*

When there is a soul seeking for light, and a messenger
willing to accept any opportunity to speak for Christ, a
meeting is certain to be arranged. So it was with Peter
and Cornelius. An extraordinary gathering it surely was!
The Roman soldier had calculated the time that Peter
would arrive and had invited to his home a large number
of his relatives and friends. Peter was returning from
Joppa with the three messengers, but was also accompanied by six Jewish Christians who might serve as witnesses
of the events which would follow. Cornelius was ready to
worship the messenger whom heaven had sent with the
good news of salvation; but Peter assured his host that he
claimed no superhuman character and that, while a Jew,
he had learned to regard no man as "common or unclean."
Cornelius then explained the extraordinary circumstances
which had led him to summon Peter and concluded with
these striking words: "Now therefore we are all here
present in the sight of God, to hear all things that have
been commanded thee of the Lord."

Surely this paragraph of the story contains two lessons
for each member of the modern church: First, what effort
is each making to secure for some messenger of Christ
such an audience as Cornelius prepared for Peter? Cannot each calculate with exactness some time and place

where the gospel is to be preached, and is it not possible to bring thither one's relatives and friends? Second, when present in a place of worship, cannot each be prepared to say, "We are all here present"—all, family and friends, mind as well as body—"in the sight of God"—not to be seen by others, not conscious so much of others as of the presence of God—"to hear all things"—not to be amused or to sleep—"that have been commanded thee of the Lord"—not to listen to human conjecture or the exploiting of doubts, but to receive a positive message which is delivered in a reverent spirit and with the prophetic formula: "Thus saith the Lord." What would happen were all Christian churches filled with such audiences?

4. THE MESSAGE Ch. 10:34-43

34 And Peter opened his mouth, and said,

Of a truth I perceive that God is no respecter of persons: 35 but in every nation he that feareth him, and worketh righteousness, is acceptable to him. 36 The word which he sent unto the children of Israel, preaching good tidings of peace by Jesus Christ (he is Lord of all)—37 that saying ye yourselves know, which was published throughout all Judæa, beginning from Galilee, after the baptism which John preached; 38 even Jesus of Nazareth, how God anointed him with the Holy Spirit and with power: who went about doing good, and healing all that were oppressed of the devil; for God was with him. 39 And we are witnesses of all things which he did both in the country of the Jews, and in Jerusalem; whom also they slew, hanging him on a tree. 40 Him God raised up the third day, and gave him to be made manifest, 41 not to all the people, but unto witnesses that were chosen before of God, even to us, who ate and drank with him after he rose from the dead. 42 And he charged us to preach unto the people, and to testify that this is he who is ordained of God to be the Judge of the living and the dead. 43 To him bear all the prophets witness, that through his name every one that believeth on him shall receive remission of sins.

Peter found time to deliver only part of the message he had in mind, only his introduction and theme. (Ch. 11:15.) His opening sentence has been strangely misunderstood. Peter did not mean that Cornelius was already saved and that in all nations men like Cornelius are saved with no knowledge of Christ, but that through Christ men of all nations can be saved even though they are not Jews. Peter had learned that men like Cornelius were "acceptable" to God in the sense that they could be saved when the gospel was presented; Peter had yet to learn that a depraved Gentile could likewise be saved, and not merely the pious, godly, and devout.

The speaker proceeded to make plain the way of salvation; he told the story of the life and works of Jesus, of his crucifixion and resurrection, and his coming again as Judge; and then he exclaimed: "To him bear all the prophets witness, that through his name every one that believeth on him shall receive remission of sins." Thus in a single sentence he declared the means of salvation—the name of Christ, that is, all Christ is revealed to be as a Savior and Lord; the universality of salvation to "every one that believeth"; the condition of salvation—belief in Christ; and also, the nature of salvation—"remission of sins"—for thus begins the experience which issues in life eternal. Surely in this message is found a model for the gospel preacher of every age, and perhaps no age has had a greater need of such clear testimony than the present.

5. THE MIRACLE   Ch. 10:44-48

44 While Peter yet spake these words, the Holy Spirit fell on all them that heard the word. 45 And they of the circumcision that believed were amazed, as many as came with Peter, because that on the Gentiles also was poured out the gift of the Holy Spirit. 46 For they heard them speak with tongues, and magnify God. Then answered Peter, 47 Can any man forbid the water, that these should not be baptized, who have received the Holy Spirit as well as we? 48 And he commanded them to be baptized in the name of Jesus Christ. Then prayed they him to tarry certain days.

In the midst of his sermon Peter was interrupted. The Holy Spirit came upon his hearers and they began to "speak with tongues" and to "magnify God." What happened was simply this: as Cornelius and his friends heard the message concerning the saving power of Christ, they accepted Christ and were filled at once with the Spirit of Christ. Peter had expected to complete his sermon, to ask those present to confess their faith, to baptize those who believed, and then to lay his hands upon them that they might receive the miraculous gifts of the Holy Spirit. In this typical case of Gentile conversion the program was cut short by the gift of the Holy Spirit. The lesson is obvious: the work of the Holy Spirit is independent of confession or baptism or the imposition of apostolic hands; nor need there be an interval of time between the acceptance of Christ and the reception of his Spirit in all the fullness of his power. The normal process is exactly this: while a preacher is still proclaiming the gospel message, the hearer yields himself to Christ, a new life is imparted to him, and he is empowered and possessed by the Spirit of his Lord. Of course there must be a confession of faith in the rite of baptism, the new life must develop, and there must be repeated "refillings" of the Spirit; but the essential experience is the yielding of the heart to Christ and the consequent transforming of life by the power of his abiding Spirit. Miracles may no longer attend this experience; they were granted in this instance as a divine authentication of the conversion of Gentiles to faith in Christ and to a new life in him.

6. THE MEMBERS OF THE CHURCH   Ch. 11:1-18

1 Now the apostles and the brethren that were in Judæa heard that the Gentiles also had received the word of God.

2 And when Peter was come up to Jerusalem, they that were of the circumcision contended with him, 3 saying, Thou wentest in to men uncircumcised, and didst eat with them. 4 But Peter began, and expounded the matter *unto them in order, saying, 5 I was in the city of Joppa praying: and in a trance I saw a vision, a certain vessel descending, as it were a great sheet let down from heaven by four corners; and it came even unto me: 6 upon which when I had fastened mine eyes, I considered, and saw the fourfooted beasts of the earth and wild beasts and creeping things and birds of the heaven. 7 And I heard also a voice saying unto me, Rise, Peter; kill and eat. 8 But I said, Not so, Lord: for nothing common or unclean hath ever entered into my mouth. 9 But a voice answered the second time out of heaven, What God hath cleansed, make not thou common. 10 And this was done thrice: and all were drawn up again into heaven. 11 And behold, forthwith three men stood before the house in which we were, having been sent from Cæsarea unto me. 12 And the Spirit bade me go with them, making no distinction. And these six brethren also accompanied me; and we entered into the man's house: 13 and he told us how he had seen the angel standing in his house, and saying, Send to Joppa, and fetch Simon, whose surname is Peter; 14 who shall speak unto thee words, whereby thou shalt be saved, thou and all thy house. 15 And as I began to speak, the Holy Spirit fell on them, even as on us at the beginning. 16 And I remembered the word of the Lord, how he said, John indeed baptized with water; but ye shall be baptized in the Holy Spirit. 17 If then God gave unto them the like gift as* he did *also unto us, when we believed on the Lord Jesus Christ, who was I, that I could withstand God? 18 And when they heard these things, they held their peace, and glorified God, saying, Then to the Gentiles also hath God granted repentance unto life.*

The news of the conversion of Gentiles was not slow in reaching Jerusalem, and the disciples at once called Peter to account for the part he had played in the incident. There is little suggestion here of papal infallibility as belonging to Simon Peter; the early church was democratic.

The charge against the apostle was not that he had preached to Gentiles—no one would have objected to that —but he had been entertained by Gentiles and had eaten with them; that was his startling offense.

Peter rehearsed the whole story, and had with him as witnesses the six Jewish Christians from Joppa who had also accompanied him to the home of Cornelius. His narrative took the form, however, of a logical argument. First, he related his vision of the vessel let down from heaven, and its divine message that what God made clean men should not regard as unclean.

Secondly, he told them that God had set his seal upon the actual cleansing and conversion of the Gentiles by the miraculous gifts of his Holy Spirit. Thirdly, he assured the church that these words of Christ had come to have for him a new meaning: "John indeed baptized with water; but ye shall be baptized in the Holy Spirit." If these men had been baptized with the Spirit, was it wrong to have administered to them the lesser baptism of water? Thus the word, "ye," used by Christ, had been divinely expanded; it had been shown to include Gentiles.

What, then, was Peter's conclusion? Nothing less startling than this, that men who are truly cleansed and filled with the Spirit should be treated as brothers and recognized as members of the body of Christ. So unanswerable were the arguments, so convincing the facts, that the objectors were satisfied: "They held their peace, and glorified God, saying, Then to the Gentiles also hath God granted repentance unto life."

It is true that others, who did not hear this testimony of Peter, subsequently caused trouble in the church, as they insisted that Gentiles who became Christians must observe the Mosaic ritual in order to be saved, or at least to be on an equality with Jewish Christians. To determine this question the first church council was called at Jerusalem.

It is likewise true that some members of the Christian church today wish to regard class and race and social distinctions in a spirit quite contrary to the attitude of brotherhood and equality shown by Peter as he admitted the first Gentiles into the fellowship of the Christian church.

E. THE MISSION OF BARNABAS Ch. 11:19-30

19 They therefore that were scattered abroad upon the tribulation that arose about Stephen travelled as far as Phœnicia, and Cyprus, and Antioch, speaking the word to none save only to Jews. 20 But there were some of them, men of Cyprus and Cyrene, who, when they were come to Antioch, spake unto the Greeks also, preaching the Lord Jesus. 21 And the hand of the Lord was with them: and a great number that believed turned unto the Lord. 22 And the report concerning them came to the ears of the church which was in Jerusalem: and they sent forth Barnabas as far as Antioch: 23 who, when he was come, and had seen the grace of God, was glad; and he exhorted them all, that with purpose of heart they would cleave unto the Lord: 24 for he was a good man, and full of the Holy Spirit and of faith: and much people was added unto the Lord. 25 And he went forth to Tarsus to seek for Saul; 26 and when he had found him, he brought him unto Antioch. And it came to pass, that even for a whole year they were gathered together with the church, and taught much people; and that the disciples were called Christians first in Antioch.

27 Now in these days there came down prophets from Jerusalem unto Antioch. 28 And there stood up one of them named Agabus, and signified by the Spirit that there should be a great famine over all the world: which came to pass in the days of Claudius. 29 And the disciples, every man according to his ability, determined to send relief unto the brethren that dwelt in Judæa: 30 which also they did, sending it to the elders by the hand of Barnabas and Saul.

The importance of these events may be summarized in large measure by four brief statements: A Christian church is organized among Gentiles; a new center is established for witnessing; a new evangelist is called to active service; a new name is given to believers.

The most prominent actor in these scenes is Barnabas. The occasion of his visit to Antioch was the success attained by certain Christians who had been driven from Jerusalem by the persecution which arose in connection with the death of Stephen; these men, natives of Cyprus and Cyrene, whose vision had been broadened by the teachings of the martyr, when they reached Antioch, preached the gospel not only to Jews but also to Greek Gentiles. Their testimony was so blessed that a great multitude accepted Christ. The word reached the church in Jerusalem and Barnabas was dispatched to investigate the nature of the work and to confirm the new converts. The character of this messenger has been revealed earlier in the narrative; he was a "son of consolation," a generous-hearted, broad-minded man, a native of Cyprus, and thus the more likely to approve of the work done by the "men of Cyprus."

Barnabas rejoiced to see the work of grace which God had wrought in the heathen city, and he was glad to welcome the new converts as brethren in Christ. His presence resulted in strengthening the believers and in a great extension of the work, for, as Luke tells us, "he was a good man, and full of the Holy Spirit and of faith." One who is full of faith is sure to be full of the Holy Spirit, and one who is filled with the Spirit will be truly "good."

The visit of Barnabas resulted not only in the rapid growth of the church but also in securing a new evangelist who became the great apostle to the Gentile world. Realizing his need of help in the leadership and guidance of the church, Barnabas went to Tarsus and invited Saul to come to Antioch and to assist him in the work. This invitation was an act of unselfishness and of discernment. Barnabas must have realized that if he were associated with such a master mind as Saul, he himself would soon sink into a place of secondary importance; but his supreme concern was the success of the cause of Christ, and he recognized the surpassing qualifications possessed by Saul for work in a Greek city. The Lord had given to Saul preparation for a worldwide witness, and he used the generous invitation of Barnabas as the means of starting upon his course the greatest missionary of all the ages. Next, if second, to accomplishing a notable task for Christ and his church, is the privilege of being allowed to play the part of a Barnabas and to introduce a great worker to his task.

That "the disciples were called Christians first in Antioch" is popularly attributed to the derision or ridicule of their enemies; the narrative seems to indicate that it was due to the teaching of Barnabas and Saul; but whatever its source the new name is full of significance. It indicates that the teaching of the apostles and the lives of the believers found their sum and their center in Christ, and further, that the church was no longer regarded as a local institution belonging to Jews and to Jerusalem, but was a body of believers whose sphere of influence was the whole wide world.

For this work of universal evangelization, Antioch was a fit center. The city was the third in the Empire, outranked only by Rome and Alexandria; it contained a mixed population, and was connected with both the East and the West by great routes of commerce and trade. It lay outside of Palestine; its church would be free from Jewish control and prejudices. A better base for missionary operations could not have been found. Antioch was the natural door to the Greco-Roman world; and the establishment there of a strong Gentile church was a step of prime importance in the preparations providentially being made for the carrying of the gospel "unto the uttermost part of the earth."

The church at Antioch, however, was not separate from the church in Jerusalem; both formed one body in Christ. This abiding unity of the church ever needs to be emphasized. It was recognized when Barnabas was sent to Antioch; it was further indicated on his return to Jerusalem. Anticipating a predicted famine, the Christians of Antioch "determined to send relief unto the brethren that dwelt in Judæa: which also they did, sending it . . . by the hand of Barnabas and Saul." This gift, like the community of goods practiced at Pentecost, was a spontaneous act of Christian generosity, but it showed to the believers in Jerusalem that the work of grace at Antioch was genuine and it united Jewish and Gentile believers in the bonds of a common spiritual life. A new group of Christians had come into being, but it formed a part of the one universal church.

F. THE PERSECUTION OF HEROD Ch. 12

1 Now about that time Herod the king put forth his hands to afflict certain of the church. 2 And he killed James the brother of John with the sword. 3 And when he saw that it pleased the Jews, he proceeded to seize Peter also. And those were the days of unleavened bread. 4 And when he had taken him, he put him in prison, and delivered him to four quaternions of soldiers to guard him; intending after the Passover to bring him forth to the people. 5 Peter therefore was kept in the prison: but prayer was made earnestly of the church unto God for him. 6 And when Herod was about to bring him forth, the same night Peter was sleeping between two soldiers, bound with two chains: and guards before the door kept the prison. 7 And behold, an angel of the Lord stood by him, and a light shined in the cell: and he smote Peter on the side, and awoke him, saying, Rise up quickly. And his chains fell off from his hands. 8 And the angel said unto him, Gird thyself, and bind on thy sandals. And he did so. And he saith unto him, Cast thy garment about thee, and follow me. 9 And he went out, and followed; and he knew not that it was true which was done by the angel, but thought he saw a vision. 10 And when they were past the first and the second guard, they came unto the iron gate that leadeth into the city; which opened to them of its own accord: and they went out, and passed on through one

*street; and straightway the angel departed from him.
11 And when Peter was come to himself, he said, Now I
know of a truth, that the Lord hath sent forth his angel
and delivered me out of the hand of Herod, and from all
the expectation of the people of the Jews. 12 And when
he had considered the thing, he came to the house of Mary
the mother of John whose surname was Mark; where many
were gathered together and were praying. 13 And when
he knocked at the door of the gate, a maid came to answer, named Rhoda. 14 And when she knew Peter's voice,
she opened not the gate for joy, but ran in, and told that
Peter stood before the gate. 15 And they said unto her,
Thou art mad. But she confidently affirmed that it was
even so. And they said, It is his angel. 16 But Peter continued knocking: and when they had opened, they saw
him, and were amazed. 17 But he, beckoning unto them
with the hand to hold their peace, declared unto them how
the Lord had brought him forth out of the prison. And
he said, Tell these things unto James, and to the brethren.
And he departed, and went to another place. 18 Now as
soon as it was day, there was no small stir among the soldiers, what was become of Peter. 19 And when Herod
had sought for him, and found him not, he examined the
guards, and commanded that they should be put to death.
And he went down from Judæa to Cæsarea, and tarried
there.*

*20 Now he was highly displeased with them of Tyre and
Sidon: and they came with one accord to him, and, having
made Blastus the king's chamberlain their friend, they
asked for peace, because their country was fed from the
king's country. 21 And upon a set day Herod arrayed
himself in royal apparel, and sat on the throne, and made
an oration unto them. 22 And the people shouted, saying,
The voice of a god, and not of a man. 23 And immediately an angel of the Lord smote him, because he gave not
God the glory: and he was eaten of worms, and gave up
the ghost.*

24 But the word of God grew and multiplied.

*25 And Barnabas and Saul returned from Jerusalem,
when they had fulfilled their ministration, taking with them
John whose surname was Mark.*

The position, as well as the contents of this chapter, should be carefully observed. It closes that section of The Acts which tells how the church was prepared to undertake the task of evangelizing the Gentile world; it shows the mad hatred felt by the Jews against the Christians, and their utter rejection of the gospel, so that if the gospel is to be preached it must be preached to the Gentiles; it also shows the protection which the Lord will give his witnesses as they go into all the world with his message. The hatred appears in the persecution which Herod undertook merely to please the Jews; the divine protection appears in the deliverance of Peter and in the death of Herod.

This Herod Agrippa had acquired the realm of his grandfather, "Herod the Great," and like him was cruel, bloodthirsty, vain, and fond of magnificent display. He was always eager to win favor with the Jews, and so, learning of their hatred against the church, he beheaded James and arrested Peter, intending shortly to execute him also. This James was the apostle who had been so closely associated with Jesus, and with Peter and John. For him his mother had asked a chief place in the Kingdom. This our Lord did not definitely refuse; but he declared it must be deserved, and he warned James that he must expect to share his cup of suffering. Of that cup James tasted the bitter dregs and was the first among the apostles of Christ to win the martyr's crown.

The deliverance of Peter is related with graphic vividness and with minute detail. Once before he had escaped from prison in Jerusalem; now he is guarded with peculiar care; sixteen soldiers are detailed, four for each watch. However, by supernatural power and under the guidance of an angel, he finds himself free to leave the dungeon and to join the group of Christians who have met for prayer in the home of Mary, the mother of Mark.

The very fact of such divine intervention indicates how serious was the crisis for the church, and how great its peril; but the deliverance was a clear declaration that while a civil power might persecute, and while Christians might be compelled to suffer, no government can ever destroy the church of Christ.

It has often been observed as true to nature that when Peter appeared in safety, in response to the prayers of the disciples, they did not believe that it could be Peter, but thought that it must be his disembodied spirit. The servant maid, Rhoda, alone seems to have had real faith. While the story rebukes our too common unbelief, it may encourage us to know that God often grants gracious answers to prayers of quite imperfect faith.

The execution of the guards is a proof of the reality of the miraculous deliverance of the apostle, for it shows that Peter had escaped, and it is an additional intimation of the cruelty of the king, for a fair investigation might have relieved these guards from blame.

The divine judgment visited upon Herod is declared to have been, not for his persecution of the church, but because "he gave not God the glory." As a civil ruler he owed his position to God and was accountable to him; his abuse of power, both in condemning innocent men and in gratification of his personal vanity, was treason to the supreme Ruler. It is a tragic picture: the king, clothed in a robe of silver sheen, seated upon a throne and accepting divine honors, is suddenly smitten with a loathsome disease and is "eaten of worms." It is all pitiful enough; but what Christian in Jerusalem would not regard Herod's fate as a divine retribution for his attempt to destroy the church of the living God? Surely two great leaders who had been in the Holy City during these fateful days returned to Antioch with a new confidence that the living Christ would protect his witnesses; these men were Barnabas and Saul, who were about to be sent out by the church to begin the work of evangelizing the vast provinces of the Roman world.

III
THE EXTENSION
OF THE CHURCH

THE WITNESS UNTO THE UTTERMOST
PART OF THE EARTH
Chs. 13 to 28

A. PAUL'S FIRST MISSIONARY JOURNEY
Chs. 13; 14

1. PAUL IN CYPRUS   Ch. 13:1-12

1 Now there were at Antioch, in the church that was
there, *prophets and teachers, Barnabas, and Symeon that
was called Niger, and Lucius of Cyrene and Manaen the
foster-brother of Herod the tetrarch, and Saul. 2 And as
they ministered to the Lord, and fasted, the Holy Spirit
said, Separate me Barnabas and Saul for the work whereunto I have called them. 3 Then, when they had fasted
and prayed and laid their hands on them, they sent them
away.*

*4 So they, being sent forth by the Holy Spirit, went down
to Seleucia; and from thence they sailed to Cyprus. 5 And
when they were at Salamis, they proclaimed the word of
God in the synagogues of the Jews: and they had also John
as their attendant. 6 And when they had gone through the
whole island unto Paphos, they found a certain sorcerer, a
false prophet, a Jew, whose name was Bar-Jesus; 7 who
was with the proconsul, Sergius Paulus, a man of understanding. The same called unto him Barnabas and Saul,
and sought to hear the word of God. 8 But Elymas the
sorcerer (for so is his name by interpretation) withstood
them, seeking to turn aside the proconsul from the faith.
9 But Saul, who is also called Paul, filled with the Holy*

Spirit, fastened his eyes on him, 10 and said, O full of all guile and all villany, thou son of the devil, thou enemy of all righteousness, wilt thou not cease to pervert the right ways of the Lord? 11 And now, behold, the hand of the Lord is upon thee, and thou shalt be blind, not seeing the sun for a season. And immediately there fell on him a mist and a darkness; and he went about seeking some to lead him by the hand. 12 Then the proconsul, when he saw what was done, believed, being astonished at the teaching of the Lord.

When Barnabas and Saul set sail for Cyprus from Seleucia, the seaport of old Antioch, the voyage probably was of no interest to the world of their day, but the first step had been taken in a movement which has changed the course of human history and will have a vital influence upon generations yet unborn. From Cyprus they crossed the sea to Perga, passed northward over the Taurus Mountains to Antioch in Pisidia, then eastward to Iconium, to Lystra, and to Derbe, then retracing their steps and circling the province of Cilicia, they sailed from Attalia to rejoin their friends in Antioch. They had accomplished a journey of some twelve hundred miles; and through these messengers the church had begun the enterprise for which she was specially commissioned by her Lord. It is true that some sixteen years had elapsed since the commission was given; but now at last, by deliberate action, a company of Christians had sent forth their representatives to carry the gospel to the Gentile world. The work done by the apostles was not in every detail parallel to that of modern missions, yet its essential features were the same and they illustrate and enforce missionary methods and principles which are valid and vital today.

For instance, the opening sentences of the story (vs. 1-3) tell us that the missionary enterprise obviously demands that the church at home must be spiritual, prayerful, self-denying, carefully instructed in revealed truth, and deeply concerned in the work abroad. These early Christians

did not seem to be much affected by the argument that
"there are heathen enough at home"; in Antioch there
were a half million pagans when the Holy Spirit said:
"Separate me Barnabas and Saul for the work whereunto
I have called them."

As to the missionaries, it is evident that the men chosen
were the strongest, mentally and spiritually, that could be
found; they were selected by the Holy Spirit, but the
church recognized their divine call and set its seal of approval upon them by the solemn rite of ordination, and
by sending them forth as its representatives.

The experiences of the apostles in Paphos may illustrate
the opposition which missionaries must encounter.   Barnabas and Saul may have selected Cyprus as their first
field of labor because it was easily accessible by sea, on
the natural trade route, and only one hundred miles distant; then again it was the home of Barnabas; further,
the population contained many Jews, and some Christians
were already there.   For whatever reasons, they voyaged
to Salamis, and after a brief stay crossed the island by the
Roman road to Paphos, some one hundred miles to the
west.

Here was a city which was a true miniature of the world
which the missionaries were to attempt to evangelize.   The
three elements, Greek, Roman, and Jewish, were all present.   It was the center of the licentious worship of Venus,
and an example of Greek culture and moral corruption; it
was the home of Sergius Paulus, the governor of the province, a man of high character, and a representative of the
Roman government which was to give protection to the
infant church; but there too was "a certain sorcerer, a
false prophet, a Jew, whose name was Bar-Jesus," a type
of that selfish and degenerate element of the Jews which
was everywhere to oppose the work of the apostles.

As the sorcerer attempts to dissuade Sergius Paulus
from the Christian faith, Saul sees in him an agent of Satan
and pronounces upon him a solemn judgment by which

he is smitten with blindness for a time. The victory of the apostles is complete. The governor believes, being astonished not so much by the miracle as by the marvelous teaching concerning Christ. Thus the messengers of the gospel are prepared to expect bitter antagonism but certain triumph.

From this time forward the name Saul is displaced by that of Paul, in designating the apostle; probably both names were always his, one Hebrew and one Roman, and the latter is now used as more acceptable to the Roman world, as that of a Roman citizen who is to move as a flaming evangel through the Roman provinces. It is no less interesting that henceforward the order is reversed, and we usually read, not of Barnabas and Saul, but of Paul and Barnabas. The place of leadership seems to have been assumed by the one who was to be known in coming years as "the great apostle to the Gentiles."

The success in Paphos may suggest that the gospel message is to be confined to no class or caste; "not many noble" may be called, but the first convert to be named in missionary history is Sergius Paulus, the Roman deputy of Cyprus.

2. PAUL AT ANTIOCH OF PISIDIA   Ch. 13:13-52

13 Now Paul and his company set sail from Paphos and came to Perga in Pamphylia: and John departed from them and returned to Jerusalem. 14 But they, passing through from Perga, came to Antioch of Pisidia; and they went into the synagogue on the sabbath day, and sat down. 15 And after the reading of the law and the prophets the rulers of the synagogue sent unto them, saying, Brethren, if ye have any word of exhortation for the people, say on. 16 And Paul stood up, and beckoning with the hand said,

Men of Israel, and ye that fear God, hearken: 17 The God of this people Israel chose our fathers, and exalted the people when they sojourned in the land of Egypt, and with a high arm led he them forth out of it. 18 And for about the time of forty years as a nursing-father bare he them in the wilderness. 19 And when he had destroyed seven nations in the land of Canaan, he gave them their land for an inheritance, for about four hundred and fifty years: 20 and after these things he gave them judges until Samuel the prophet. 21 And afterward they asked for a king: and God gave unto them Saul the son of Kish, a man of the tribe of Benjamin, for the space of forty years. 22 And when he had removed him, he raised up David to be their king; to whom also he bare witness and said, I have found David the son of Jesse, a man after my heart, who shall do all my will. 23 Of this man's seed hath God according to promise brought unto Israel a Saviour, Jesus; 24 when John had first preached before his coming the baptism of repentance to all the people of Israel. 25 And as John was fulfilling his course, he said, What suppose ye that I am? I am not he. But behold, there cometh one after me the shoes of whose feet I am not worthy to unloose. 26 Brethren, children of the stock of Abraham, and those among you that fear God, to us is the word of this salvation sent forth. 27 For they that dwell in Jerusalem, and their rulers, because they knew him not, nor the voices of the prophets which are read every sabbath, fulfilled them by condemning him. 28 And though they found no cause of death in him, yet asked they of Pilate that he should be slain. 29 And when they had fulfilled all things that were written of him, they took him down from the tree, and laid him in a tomb. 30 But God raised him from the dead: 31 and he was seen for many days of them that came up with him from Galilee to Jerusalem, who are now his witnesses unto the people. 32 And we bring you good tidings of the promise made unto the fathers, 33 that God hath fulfilled the same unto our children, in that he raised up Jesus; as also it is written in the second psalm, Thou art my Son, this day have I begotten thee. 34 And as concerning that he raised him up from the dead, now no more to return to corruption, he hath spoken on this wise, I will give you the holy and sure blessings of David. 35 Because he saith also in another psalm, Thou wilt not give thy Holy One to see corruption. 36 For David, after he had in his own generation served the counsel of God, fell asleep, and was laid unto his fathers, and saw corruption: 37 but he whom

God raised up saw no corruption. *38 Be it known unto you therefore, brethren, that through this man is proclaimed unto you remission of sins: 39 and by him every one that believeth is justified from all things, from which ye could not be justified by the law of Moses. 40 Beware therefore, lest that come upon you which is spoken in the prophets: 41 Behold, ye despisers, and wonder, and perish;*

For I work a work in your days,

A work which ye shall in no wise believe, if one declare it unto you.

42 And as they went out, they besought that these words might be spoken to them the next sabbath. 43 Now when the synagogue broke up, many of the Jews and of the devout proselytes followed Paul and Barnabas; who, speaking to them, urged them to continue in the grace of God.

44 And the next sabbath almost the whole city was gathered together to hear the word of God. 45 But when the Jews saw the multitudes, they were filled with jealousy, and contradicted the things which were spoken by Paul, and blasphemed. 46 And Paul and Barnabas spake out boldly, and said, It was necessary that the word of God should first be spoken to you. Seeing ye thrust it from you, and judge yourselves unworthy of eternal life, lo, we turn to the Gentiles. 47 For so hath the Lord commanded us, saying,

I have set thee for a light of the Gentiles,

That thou shouldest be for salvation unto the uttermost part of the earth.

48 And as the Gentiles heard this, they were glad, and glorified the word of God: and as many as were ordained to eternal life believed. 49 And the word of the Lord was spread abroad throughout all the region. 50 But the Jews urged on the devout women of honorable estate, and the chief men of the city, and stirred up a persecution against Paul and Barnabas, and cast them out of their borders. 51 But they shook off the dust of their feet against them, and came unto Iconium. 52 And the disciples were filled with joy and with the Holy Spirit.

This section sets forth the missionary message for all times and lands. Circumstances demand minor variations, but the essence is ever the same. Paul and his party have crossed the Mediterranean from Paphos to Perga. At the latter place John Mark has deserted his friends and returned to Jerusalem. The fearless missonaries have climbed the steep passes of the Taurus Mountains and reached Pisidian Antioch on the high tableland of central Asia Minor. There on the Sabbath they have gone to the Jewish synagogue, and when invited to speak, Paul delivers his first recorded sermon. He proves from sacred history that God has always provided for his chosen people, and assures his hearers that these gifts have culminated in Jesus, the Savior of Israel; that Jesus is such a Savior he argues from the testimony of John the Baptist, from the rejection of Jesus which fulfilled the prediction of the prophets, and chiefly from the resurrection, which is attested by living witnesses, and which was foretold in notable passages of The Psalms. He closes his address with an appeal to accept the forgiveness of sins which this Savior can secure, and with a warning against unbelief, taken from the Old Testament.

It should be noticed, then, that according to the example of Paul, gospel preaching consists in presenting the crucified and risen Christ as the Savior from sin, and in appealing for proof to living witnesses and to the inspired Word.

As a result of the sermon, Paul was urged to preach again on the Sabbath following; but when the day arrived and the Jews saw that the whole city was thronging to hear Paul, they were moved with envy, they contradicted Paul and "blasphemed." Then Paul bodily declared his intention of turning to the Gentiles and defended his course by an apt quotation of Scripture. By the Gentiles his message was gladly received, yet not by all. Luke intends his readers to understand that in no place will there be universal acceptance of the gospel, either by Gentiles or Jews; only "as many as were ordained to eternal life believed." Even the apparent popularity of the missionaries was but temporary. The Jews aroused the whole city against the apostles and they were compelled to flee to Iconium; but they went with joy. Opposition and persecution are the continual experiences of missionaries, but the Lord is with them, and they rejoice that sinners are being saved.

3. PAUL AT ICONIUM, LYSTRA, AND DERBE   Ch. 14

1 And it came to pass in Iconium that they entered together into the synagogue of the Jews, and so spake that a great multitude both of Jews and of Greeks believed. 2 But the Jews that were disobedient stirred up the souls of the Gentiles, and made them evil affected against the brethren. 3 Long time therefore they tarried there speaking boldly in the Lord, who bare witness unto the word of his grace, granting signs and wonders to be done by their hands. 4 But the multitude of the city was divided; and part held with the Jews, and part with the apostles. 5 And when there was made an onset both of the Gentiles and of the Jews with their rulers, to treat them shamefully and to stone them, 6 they became aware of it, and fled unto the cities of Lycaonia, Lystra and Derbe, and the region round about: 7 and there they preached the gospel.

8 And at Lystra there sat a certain man, impotent in his feet, a cripple from his mother's womb, who never had walked. 9 The same heard Paul speaking: who, fastening his eyes upon him, and seeing that he had faith to be made whole, 10 said with a loud voice, Stand upright on thy feet. And he leaped up and walked. 11 And when the multitude saw what Paul had done, they lifted up their voice, saying in the speech of Lycaonia, The gods are come down to us in the likeness of men. 12 And they called Barnabas, Jupiter; and Paul, Mercury, because he was the chief speaker. 13 And the priest of Jupiter whose temple was before the city, brought oxen and garlands unto the gates, and would have done sacrifice with the multitudes. 14 But when the apostles, Barnabas and Paul, heard of it, they rent their garments, and sprang forth among the mulitude, crying out 15 and saying, Sirs, why do ye these things? We also are men of like passions with you, and bring you good tidings, that ye should turn from these vain things unto a living God, who made the heaven and the earth and the sea, and all that in them is:　16 who in the generations gone by suffered all the nations to walk in their own ways. 17 And yet he left not himself without witness, in that he did good and gave you from heaven rains and fruitful seasons, filling your hearts with food and gladness.　18 And with these sayings scarce restrained they the multitudes from doing sacrifice unto them.

19 But there came Jews thither from Antioch and Iconium: and having persuaded the multitudes, they stoned Paul, and dragged him out of the city, supposing that he was dead.　20 But as the disciples stood round about him, he rose up, and entered into the city: and on the morrow he went forth with Barnabas to Derbe.　21 And when they had preached the gospel to that city, and had made many disciples, they returned to Lystra, and to Iconium, and to Antioch, 22 confirming the souls of the disciples, exhorting them to continue in the faith, and that through many tribulations we must enter into the kingdom of God.　23 And when they had appointed for them elders in every church, and had prayed with fasting, they commended them to the Lord, on whom they had believed.　24 And they passed through Pisidia, and came to Pamphylia.　25 And when they had spoken the word in Perga, they went down to Attalia:　26 and thence they sailed to Antioch, from whence they had been committed to the grace of God for the work which they had fulfilled.　27 And when they were come, and had gathered the church together, they rehearsed all things that God had done with them, and that he had opened a door of faith unto the Gentiles.　28 And they tarried no little time with the disciples.

The course of Paul at Iconium illustrates two points of missionary strategy which might have been noted earlier in connection with this memorable journey: first, Paul went to the larger cities and there planted churches, designing to reach the outlying districts from these chief centers of influence; second, he moved along the line of least resistance and entered every open door, going first to his own countrymen in their synagogues, but when rejected

turning to the Gentiles.   Here at Iconium the opposition
was more severe than it had been at Antioch, and here by
contrast the manifestation of divine power was greater,
and "signs and wonders" were done by the hands of the
apostles.   This has often been the experience of Christian
workers; when difficulties increase, there is a comforting
revelation of the grace and mercy and goodness of God.

When a plot was formed against their lives, Paul and
Barnabas fled eastward to the Lycaonian cities of Lystra
and Derbe.   Is this the proper course for missionaries to
take in the face of danger?   This only circumstances can
determine.   At times it is best to suffer as martyrs; at other
times to seek safety and to resume work when the storm
is spent.

At Lystra, Paul gives an admirable example of the
necessary adaptation of the missionary message to the
people to whom it is presented, not in altering its essence,
but in the method of approach.   This second reported
sermon of Paul's must be compared with the first.   Its occasion is remarkably similar to that of Peter's "second
sermon."   In each case a cripple, hopelessly lame, is instantly cured, and the miracle attracts a wondering multitude.   At Lystra the people are so impressed that they
are about to offer sacrifices to the apostles as to gods;
Paul they suppose to be Mercury, and Barnabas, Jupiter.
To this excited throng of pagans Paul addresses himself.
He does not begin now by appealing to Scripture, of which
his hearers are of course totally ignorant, but by telling
them of God whose power and love are manifested in the
works of nature and providence.   In view of the goodness
of such a living and true God, Paul calls his hearers to repentance, and prepares the way for his message concerning Christ the Savior.

His message, however, is allowed to have little effect.
A mob of jealous Jews from Iconium arrive on the scene
and stir up the pagans to make common cause with them
against the apostles.   Paul is stoned, and dragged out of

the city and left as dead; but as his faithful followers stand by, they are rejoiced to see him rise and return fearlessly to the hostile city. On the morrow, however, he leaves with Barnabas for Derbe, where his preaching results in the establishing of a Christian church.

Luke now sketches hastily the return of the apostles, as they retrace their steps through Lystra, Iconium, Antioch, and Perga, and as they sail from Attalia to report to the home church by which they have been sent forth. He pauses, however, to lay stress on one essential point of missionary strategy, namely, the careful organization of the churches which have been formed on the field. Evangelization, in the case of Paul, did not consist in a mere, superficial, hasty heralding of the gospel, but in establishing a permanent work. At great personal risk he revisited the new converts, comforting them, instructing them, and seeing that "elders" were appointed for them "in every church." A proper missionary program has as its aim the establishment on the field of self-governing, self-sustaining, self-propagating churches. This was ever the purpose and the practice of Paul.

B. THE COUNCIL AT JERUSALEM
Ch. 15:1-35

1 And certain men came down from Judæa and taught the brethren, saying, Except ye be circumcised after the custom of Moses, ye cannot be saved. 2 And when Paul and Barnabas had no small dissension and questioning with them, the brethren appointed that Paul and Barnabas, and certain other of them, should go up to Jerusalem unto the apostles and elders about this question. 3 They therefore, being brought on their way by the church, passed through both Phœnicia and Samaria, declaring the conversion of the Gentiles: and they caused great joy unto all the brethren. 4 And when they were come to Jerusalem, they were received of the church and the apostles and the elders, and they rehearsed all things that God had done with them. 5 But there rose up certain of the sect of the Pharisees who

believed, saying, It is needful to circumcise them, and to
charge them to keep the law of Moses.

6 And the apostles and the elders were gathered together to consider of this matter. 7 And when there had
been much questioning, Peter rose up, and said unto them,

Brethren, ye know that a good while ago God made
choice among you, that by my mouth the Gentiles should
hear the word of the gospel, and believe. 8 And God, who
knoweth the heart, bare them witness, giving them the Holy
Spirit, even as he did unto us; 9 and he made no distinction
between us and them, cleansing their hearts by faith. 10
Now therefore why make ye trial of God, that ye should
put a yoke upon the neck of the disciples which neither
our fathers nor we were able to bear? 11 But we believe
that we shall be saved through the grace of the Lord Jesus,
in like manner as they.

12 And all the multitude kept silence; and they hearkened unto Barnabas and Paul rehearsing what signs and
wonders God had wrought among the Gentiles through
them. 13 And after they had held their peace, James answered, saying,

Brethren, hearken unto me: 14 Symeon hath rehearsed
how first God visited the Gentiles, to take out of them a
people for his name. 15 And to this agree the words of the
prophets; as it is written,

16 After these things I will return,
    And I will build again the tabernacle of David, which is
      fallen;
    And I will build again the ruins thereof,
    And I will set it up:
17 That the residue of men may seek after the Lord,
    And all the Gentiles, upon whom my name is called,
18 Saith the Lord, who maketh these things known from
      of old.
19 Wherefore my judgment is, that we trouble not them
that from among the Gentiles turn to God; 20 but that we
write unto them, that they abstain from the pollutions of
idols, and from fornication, and from what is strangled, and
from blood. 21 For Moses from generations of old hath
in every city them that preach him, being read in the synagogues every sabbath.

22 Then it seemed good to the apostles and the elders,

*with the whole church, to choose men out of their com-
pany, and send them to Antioch with Paul and Barnabas;*
namely, *Judas called Barsabbas, and Silas, chief men among
the brethren: 23 And they wrote thus by them, The apostles and the elders, brethren, unto the brethren who are of
the Gentiles in Antioch and Syria and Cilicia, greeting:
24 Forasmuch as we have heard that certain who went out
from us have troubled you with words, subverting your
souls; to whom we gave no commandment; 25 it seemed
good unto us, having come to one accord, to choose out
men and send them unto you with our beloved Barnabas
and Paul, 26 men that have hazarded their lives for the
name of our Lord Jesus Christ. 27 We have sent therefore
Judas and Silas, who themselves also shall tell you the same
things by word of mouth. 28 For it seemed good to the
Holy Spirit, and to us, to lay upon you no greater burden
than these necessary things: 29 that ye abstain from things
sacrificed to idols, and from blood, and from things
strangled, and from fornication; from which if ye keep
yourselves, it shall be well with you. Fare ye well.*

*30 So they, when they were dismissed, came down to
Antioch; and having gathered the multitude together, they
delivered the epistle. 31 And when they had read it, they
rejoiced for the consolation. 32 And Judas and Silas, being themselves also prophets, exhorted the brethren with
many words, and confirmed them. 33 And after they had
spent some time there, they were dismissed in peace from
the brethren unto those that had sent them forth. 35 But
Paul and Barnabas tarried in Antioch, teaching and preaching the word of the Lord, with many others also.*

It was in the church at Antioch that the problem arose
which caused Paul to be sent to Jerusalem as a delegate
to "the first council" of the Christian church. It is commonly remembered that the disciples were called Christians first at Antioch. The church of that city had,
however, a more honorable distinction; it was the first missionary church, and it became the radiating center for the
evangelization of the Gentile world. A missionary spirit
is an enviable distinction for any church today.

The problem was caused by missionary activity. Missions are always creating problems; they are demanding men and money and thought and prayer; they require the readjustment of personal plans and cooperation among men of divergent opinions. Dead churches have no problems. It was the success of Paul's first missionary journey and the great numbers of Gentile converts, which occasioned so great a divergence of opinion between certain Christians of Antioch and of Jerusalem that it was deemed necessary to send Paul and Barnabas and others with them to Jerusalem to consult with the members of the mother church. The problem concerned the missionary message. This is the fundamental and the supreme question in all modern missionary enterprise. All then agreed that the gospel message centered in the one word "salvation." They interpreted that word in its spiritual sense. They did not mean by it merely an improved social condition, but a state of the soul and a relation to God. It meant deliverance from the guilt, power, and presence of sin, and a life of holiness and service. All agreed that it was attained by faith in Christ, but while Paul had preached, on his missionary journey, that it was by faith alone, certain members of the Jerusalem church insisted that it also was necessary to keep the law of Moses. Was Paul's missionary message correct? What must one do to be saved?

The difficulty did not seem great to Paul. He felt certain that he was right. On his journey to Jerusalem he gave great joy by announcing the salvation of Gentiles who had been converted by means of his message of "faith in Christ." In the minds of the converted Pharisees, however, the difficulty was very great indeed. Most serious of all was the fact that the Scriptures seemed to be on their side. The Old Testament required and in no place abrogated the ceremonial law. This law our Savior himself kept with scrupulous care. How could its obligations be omitted from the missionary message? How could the freedom from the law which Paul preached be reconciled with the authority of Scripture? How shall we reconcile, today, faith and works, freedom and necessity, grace and law?

After a private conference of leaders an open discussion is held. Peter naturally speaks first. He argues from the case of Cornelius and his friends, whom the advocates of the law seem to have forgotten. These people were saved without any legal observance, and even before Christian baptism. Further, Peter insists, the law is too heavy a yoke for anyone to bear. Who among modern Christians has ever kept the law as it was interpreted by the Master in his Sermon on the Mount? Lastly, as Peter contends, we and all others must be saved wholly by grace through faith in Christ. There is no other way of salvation.

Paul is the next speaker. He tells the story of his recent missionary journey and reports the conversion and the new life of multitudes of Gentiles who have been saved without the least knowledge of the ceremonial law. This was a stubborn fact. The results of missions are today the best proof of the truth of the gospel message.

James is the last speaker. He shows that, after all, the Scriptures do agree with the gospel message, and had predicted that, through a Prince who was to arise in the house of David, salvation was to come to Gentiles, who were to be saved as such and without observing the law of Moses.

The decision, suggested by James, and accepted by the council, included three points: (1) Liberty (ch. 15:19); the law of Moses need not be kept, and could not be a ground of salvation. This decision was the "Magna Charta" of Christian liberty. (Gal. 2:15-21.) (2) Purity (ch. 15:20); liberty is not license, but a life of holiness, by faith in Christ. (Gal. 5:13-26.) (3) Charity; in matters of indifference let us not needlessly offend those who prefer to observe certain forms and ceremonies. (Gal. 6:2.)

A circular letter, announcing this decision and sent in the name of the whole church, gave great joy to the local congregations and resulted in a spirit of unity and harmony and peace. Only such a union of Christians as is based on the acceptance of the fundamental doctrines of grace can promise missionary success and the wide proclamation of a true gospel message.

C. PAUL'S SECOND MISSIONARY JOURNEY
Chs. 15:36 to 18:22

1. THE COMPANIONS IN TRAVEL
Chs. 15:36 to 16:5

36 And after some days Paul said unto Barnabas, Let us return now and visit the brethren in every city wherein we proclaimed the word of the Lord, and see how they fare. 37 And Barnabas was minded to take with them John also, who was called Mark. 38 But Paul thought not good to take with them him who withdrew from them from Pamphylia, and went not with them to the work. 39 And there arose a sharp contention, so that they parted asunder one from the other, and Barnabas took Mark with him, and sailed away unto Cyprus; 40 but Paul chose Silas, and went forth, being commended by the brethren to the grace of the Lord. 41 and he went through Syria and Cilicia, confirming the churches.

1 And he came also to Derbe and to Lystra: and behold, a certain disciple was there, named Timothy, the son of a Jewess that believed; but his father was a Greek. 2 The same was well reported of by the brethren that were at Lystra and Iconium. 3 Him would Paul have to go forth with him; and he took and circumcised him because of the Jews that were in those parts: for they all knew that his father was a Greek. 4 And as they went on their way through the cities, they delivered them the decrees to keep which had been ordained of the apostles and elders that were at Jerusalem. 5 So the churches were strengthened in the faith, and increased in number daily.

The notable fact in relation to Paul's second missionary journey is that it resulted in the establishment of Christian churches on the continent of Europe. These formed radiating centers for evangelistic work, and included in their influence the cities of Philippi, Thessalonica, and Corinth.

The story opens with the record of a painful incident, the separation of Paul and Barnabas. A dispute arose as to the wisdom of taking with them John Mark, who, on the former journey, had deserted them at Perga. It seems certain that Mark had been at fault, but the question was as to whether he should be forgiven and granted another trial. The more lenient view was taken by Barnabas, who was cousin to Mark and a man of gentle and sympathetic disposition. Paul was animated by his consuming zeal for the great work which he felt should not be imperiled out of regard for individual feelings and preferences. The controversy became so severe that the apostles determined to part company.

One of the most serious problems of modern missions, in fact of all Christian enterprises, is that of the personal relation of the workers. Sometimes it is necessary "to agree to disagree"; usually serious differences are as truly forgiven and forgotten as was the case, in later years, with Paul and Barnabas and Mark.

The incident is to be regretted and must have been distressing to the devoted friends whose lives had been so long intertwined; but it was overruled for the wider extension of the work. Barnabas took Mark and sailed for Cyprus, while Paul chose Silas and started overland for Cilicia. The purposes of God cannot be delayed by human frailties; if one worker fails, another is put in his place.

The successor to Mark, as the assistant of Paul, was Timothy. He was somewhat timid, diffident, and emotional, but affectionate, sincere, and devoted. He became Paul's closest friend and most constant companion, and as dear to the great apostle as a "beloved child." Paul discovered this young disciple as he revisited the cities of

Lystra and Derbe. While Timothy had been carefully instructed in the Scriptures by his Jewish mother and grandmother, his father was a Gentile and the Mosaic law had not been observed in the home. In order to avoid all offense to the Jews among whom Paul was to work, Timothy was circumcised; he was then ordained by the presbytery, and started with Paul upon the memorable journey which brought the evangelists to Europe. The whole story is a beautiful commentary upon the value of friendships and companionships in Christian service and particularly in the work on foreign fields.

2. PAUL AT PHILIPPI   Ch. 16:6-40

6 And they went through the region of Phrygia and Galatia, having been forbidden of the Holy Spirit to speak the word in Asia; 7 and when they were come over against Mysia, they assayed to go into Bithynia; and the Spirit of Jesus suffered them not; 8 and passing by Mysia, they came down to Troas. 9 And a vision appeared to Paul in the night: There was a man of Macedonia standing, beseeching him, and saying, Come over into Macedonia, and help us. 10 And when he had seen the vision, straightway we sought to go forth into Macedonia, concluding that God had called us to preach the gospel unto them.

11 Setting sail therefore from Troas, we made a straight course to Samothrace, and the day following to Neapolis; 12 and from thence to Philippi, which is a city of Macedonia, the first of the district, a Roman colony: and we were in this city tarrying certain days. 13 And on the sabbath day we went forth without the gate by a river side, where we supposed there was a place of prayer; and we sat down, and spake unto the women that were come together. 14 And a certain woman named Lydia, a seller of purple, of the city of Thyatira, one that worshipped God, heard us: whose heart the Lord opened to give heed unto the things which were spoken by Paul. 15 And when she was baptized, and her household, she besought us, saying, If ye have judged me to be faithful to the Lord, come into my house, and abide there. *And she constrained us.*

16 And it came to pass, as we were going to the place of prayer, that a certain maid having a spirit of divination met us, who brought her masters much gain by soothsaying. 17 The same following after Paul and us cried out, saying, These men are servants of the Most High God, who proclaim unto you the way of salvation. 18 And this she did for many days. But Paul, being sore troubled, turned and said to the spirit, I charge thee in the name of Jesus Christ to come out of her. And it came out that very hour.

19 But when her masters saw that the hope of their gain was gone, they laid hold on Paul and Silas, and dragged them into the marketplace before the rulers, 20 and when they had brought them unto the magistrates, they said, These men, being Jews, do exceedingly trouble our city, 21 and set forth customs which it is not lawful for us to receive, or to observe, being Romans. 22 And the multitude rose up together against them: and the magistrates rent their garments off them, and commanded to beat them with rods. 23 And when they had laid many stripes upon them, they cast them into prison, charging the jailor to keep them safely: 24 who, having received such a charge, cast them into the inner prison, and made their feet fast in the stocks. 25 But about midnight Paul and Silas were praying and singing hymns unto God, and the prisoners were listening to them; 26 and suddenly there was a great earthquake, so that the foundations of the prison-house were shaken: and immediately all the doors were opened: and every one's bands were loosed. 27 And the jailor, being roused out of sleep and seeing the prison doors open, drew his sword and was about to kill himself, supposing that the prisoners had escaped. 28 But Paul cried with a loud voice, saying, Do thyself no harm: for we are all here. 29 And he called for lights and sprang in, and, trembling for fear, fell down before Paul and Silas, 30 and brought them out and said, Sirs, what must I do to be saved? 31 And they said, Believe on the Lord Jesus, and thou shalt be saved, thou and thy house. 32 And they spake the word of the Lord unto him, with all that were in his house. 33 And he took them the same hour of the night and washed their stripes; and was baptized, he and

*all his, immediately. 34 And he brought them up into his
house, and set food before them, and rejoiced greatly, with
all his house, having believed in God.*

*35 But when it was day, the magistrates sent the ser-
jeants, saying, Let those men go. 36 And the jailor reported the words to Paul, saying, The magistrates have sent
to let you go: now therefore come forth, and go in peace.
37 But Paul said unto them, They have beaten us publicly,
uncondemned, men that are Romans, and have cast us into
prison; and do they now cast us out privily? nay verily; but
let them come themselves and bring us out. 38 And the
serjeants reported these words unto the magistrates: and
they feared when they heard that they were Romans;
39 and they came and besought them; and when they had
brought them out, they asked them to go away from the
city. 40 And they went out of the prison, and entered into
the house of Lydia: and when they had seen the brethren,
they comforted them, and departed.*

The original purpose announced by Paul was to visit
the churches he had previously established; but the horizon of his privilege and duty was unexpectedly widened.
After passing through Phrygia and Galatia, he was providentially hindered from going to Bithynia, and so he
moved westward until he reached Troas and was stopped
by the sea. It has been well said that "the stops as well
as the steps of a good man are ordered by the Lord."
Then came the vision in the night: "There was a man of
Macedonia standing, beseeching him, and saying, Come
over into Macedonia, and help us." When one is looking
for guidance and ready to obey, even a comparatively
insignificant sign may be sufficient to indicate his course;
and the historian declares: "When he had seen the vision,
straightway we sought to go forth into Macedonia, concluding that God had called us to preach the gospel unto
them."

But who is this historian who now for the first time uses
this word "we" and "us" and writes as an eyewitness?
It is almost certainly Luke, "the beloved physician," who

now joins the party, worthy leader of that loyal host of
medical missionaries who have been among the pioneers
to carry relief to suffering bodies and needy souls beyond
the seas.

The momentous voyage to Europe occupied but a few
days. The travelers landed at Neapolis and crossed the
mountains to Philippi, ten miles distant. On the plains of
Philippi, nearly a century before, the empire of the world
had been determined when Augustus and Antony defeated
Brutus and Cassius. The city was a military colony, a
miniature Rome, and in the persons who there met the
apostles are mirrored the moral and spiritual needs of the
ancient and modern world.

The first convert to be made in Philippi, and so the first
in Europe, was Lydia. She was a woman of wealth, of
intelligence, of wide experience, a seller of purple cloth,
who had come from the city of Thyatira; moreover she
was religious, godly, prayerful. Yet this woman needed
salvation, she needed Christ. Paul found her in a group
of women who had met on the Sabbath at a place of
prayer; the Lord opened her heart to believe the gospel
message, she was baptized, and received the apostles as
guests in her hospitable home. Such persons are to be
found in every land; but it is certainly not in accordance
with Scripture to insist that they are saved without the
gospel. Their moral, upright, prayerful lives are said by
some modern teachers to indicate that they already have
"the essential Christ," that they are already possessed of
a spiritual life which is quite the same as that of professed
Christians, in kind if not in degree. The case of the first
convert in Europe gives a different suggestion and sounds
a call to the church to pass by no longer in unconcern
these noble souls who are yearning for the light and peace
and life that the gospel alone can bring. The character of
Lydia reminds the reader of the Ethiopian eunuch, of Saul
of Tarsus, of Cornelius the centurion; all were good, upright, godly; yet they needed the salvation which comes

from an intelligent faith in a crucified, risen, divine Christ; and these are typical converts in the history of the early church.

If Lydia suggests the need of that which the gospel messengers can bring, so her generous act, following her conversion, symbolizes the invaluable support given by women, in all the centuries, to the cause of Christian missions. Lydia the Jewess, however, is not the common type of womanhood in heathen lands; their condition is pictured rather by the poor slave girl, "the pythoness," possessed by an evil spirit, whose distress was a source of gain to her masters. Such are either the toys or the tools of men. Their nameless agonies and anguish are the real "Macedonian cry" which the church of Christian lands should heed. Nor is their deepest distress that of outward circumstances; they need to have the evil cast out of their hearts. To the demon which possessed the degraded girl in Philippi, Paul spoke his memorable words: "I charge thee in the name of Jesus Christ to come out of her." "And it came out that very hour." The women of the Orient are not all like the slave girl; some are like Lydia; but millions are waiting for messengers who can speak to them with the confident faith felt by Paul in the omnipotent name of Christ.

The release of the girl arouses the bitter anger of her "masters"; there are men today who are willing to acquire wealth by the degradation of womanhood, and who resent as impertinent intrusion every attempt to deliver their victims from the power of sin. Thus these men regarded the action of Paul. They succeeded in having the apostles beaten and imprisoned on a false charge and without a legal trial.

The undaunted evangelists, bleeding and bruised, and confined to an inner dungeon, sang songs in the night, until God shook the prison and set his messengers free. All who oppose the forces of organized vice can expect bitter opposition, but being on the side of Christ is being on the side of omnipotence, and there is no need of despair.

The earthquake which opened the prison, the strange charge against the apostles, the salvation of which they had spoken, his own fear and sense of need, resulted in the conversion of the jailer. He is a type of the debased, depressed, degraded manhood which always needs the gospel. Not all men are like Saul and Cornelius. The jailer's ready acceptance of the message, his subsequent conduct, his immediate confession of faith, all illustrate how clearly he understood the answer which Paul gave to his eager question as to the way of salvation: "Believe on the Lord Jesus, and thou shalt be saved, thou and thy house." Surely that message is adapted to the needs of men of every class and condition.

In the morning the magistrates, moved no doubt by what had been reported to them, sent word to release Paul and Silas; but Paul insisted upon a public vindication and still further terrified the rulers by the announcement that he was a Roman citizen. The magistrates in their treatment of the apostle had thus been guilty of a serious offense. No wonder they hastened to the prison to lead forth the apostles with all deference and respect. The triumph of Paul was complete. He was willing to suffer for the sake of Christ, but he wished the civil governors to realize more fully that in persecuting men for their Christian faith they offended against the laws both of men and of God.

3. PAUL AT THESSALONICA AND BEREA
Ch. 17:1-15

1 Now when they had passed through Amphipolis and Apollonia, they came to Thessalonica, where was a synagogue of the Jews: 2 and Paul, as his custom was, went in unto them, and for three sabbath days reasoned with them from the scriptures, 3 opening and alleging that it behooved the Christ to suffer, and to rise again from the dead; and that this Jesus, whom, said he, *I proclaim unto you, is the Christ. 4 And some of them were persuaded, and consorted with Paul and Silas; and of the devout Greeks a great multitude, and of the chief women not a few. 5 But the Jews, being moved with jealousy, took unto them certain vile fellows of the rabble, and gathering a crowd, set the city on an uproar; and assaulting the house of Jason, they sought to bring them forth to the people. 6 And when they found them not, they dragged Jason and certain brethren before the rulers of the city, crying, These that have turned the world upside down are come hither also; 7 whom Jason hath received: and these all act contrary to the decrees of Cæsar, saying that there is another king, one Jesus. 8 And they troubled the multitude and the rulers of the city, when they heard these things. 9 And when they had taken security from Jason and the rest, they let them go.*

10 And the brethren immediately sent away Paul and Silas by night unto Berœa: who when they were come thither went into the synagogue of the Jews. 11 Now these were more noble than those in Thessalonica, in that they received the word with all readiness of mind, examining the scriptures daily, whether these things were so. 12 Many of them therefore believed; also of the Greek women of honorable estate, and of men, not a few. 13 But when the Jews of Thessalonica had knowledge that the word of God was proclaimed of Paul at Berœa also, they came thither likewise, stirring up and troubling the multitudes. 14 And then immediately the brethren sent forth Paul to go as far as to the sea: and Silas and Timothy abode there still. 15 But they that conducted Paul brought him as far as Athens: and receiving a commandment unto Silas and Timothy that they should come to him with all speed, they departed.

A journey of about one hundred miles southwest brought Paul to Thessalonica, and then about fifty miles farther along the same Roman road, to Berea; his stay in the former city intimates how the gospel should be preached, his experience in Berea, how it should be received.

Thessalonica, now known as Salonika, was a city of considerable size and influence; in modern times it was the second city of the Turkish Empire; and the eyes of the world have been fixed upon it recently by the events of the Great War. Strange to say, its real fame rests rather upon the visit paid to the city by a Christian missionary centuries ago and to two short letters he wrote to the church he founded there. A reference to these Thessalonian letters shows that Paul must have remained in the city somewhat longer than the "three sabbath days" to which Luke refers. This earlier period was devoted largely to work among the Jews, but several weeks more were spent in securing the Gentile converts of which the church was chiefly composed. Both The Acts and the Epistles, however, lay great stress upon the content of the message delivered by Paul. It was essentially an exposition of the Scriptures, which, after all has been said, is the most valuable form of preaching in the present day. His one theme was Jesus Christ, whom he proved to be the true Savior, the promised Messiah, and who, as the Old Testament declared, must necessarily have suffered for sin and risen from the dead. The Epistles show further the great stress laid upon the Second Coming of Christ as the glorious King.

It was this last doctrine upon which the enemies of Paul laid hold, as they aroused a mob in the city and attempted to seize the apostle. Not finding him in the home where he was being entertained, they dragged Jason, his host, before the rulers of the city, charging him with harboring men guilty of treason, men who had said, "there is another king, one Jesus." The magistrates acted with all fairness, recording the charge and releasing Jason on bail to await trial.

Paul, Silas, and Timothy made their escape by night and moved on to Berea. Here the Jews showed that they "were more noble than those in Thessalonica, in that they received the word with all readiness of mind, examining the scriptures daily, whether these things were so." Such hearers are ideal, and contrast strikingly with such as Paul met in Thessalonica, whose blind prejudice prevented them from fairly weighing the evidence for the teachings proclaimed. In religious differences the question is not so much what teachers think as what the Scriptures say. The Jews of Thessalonica, moved by envy, pursued the apostle to Berea. Enraged by the success he had attained in his new field of labor, they aroused the people and compelled him to continue his flight. Silas and Timothy, however, were left behind; Luke also seems to have remained at Philippi; but Paul took ship and sailed three hundred miles southward to Athens.

4. PAUL AT ATHENS   Ch. 17:16-34

16 Now while Paul waited for them at Athens, his spirit was provoked within him as he beheld the city full of idols. 17 So he reasoned in the synagogue with the Jews and the devout persons, and in the marketplace every day with them that met him. 18 And certain also of the Epicurean and Stoic philosophers encountered him. And some said, What would this babbler say? others, He seemeth to be a setter forth of strange gods: because he preached Jesus and the resurrection. 19 And they took hold of him, and brought him unto the Areopagus, saying, May we know what this new teaching is, which is spoken by thee? 20 For thou bringest certain strange things to our ears: we would know therefore what these things mean. 21 (Now all the Athenians and the strangers sojourning there spent their time in nothing else, but either to tell or to hear some new thing.) 22 And Paul stood in the midst of the Areopagus, and said,

Ye men of Athens, in all things I perceive that ye are very religious. 23 For as I passed along, and observed the objects of your worship, I found also an altar with this inscription, TO AN UNKNOWN GOD. What therefore ye worship in ignorance, this I set forth unto you. 24 The God that made the world and all things therein, he, being Lord of heaven and earth, dwelleth not in temples made with

*hands; 25 neither is he served by men's hands, as though
he needed anything, seeing he himself giveth to all life, and
breath, and all things; 26 and he made of one every nation
of men to dwell on all the face of the earth, having determined their appointed seasons, and the bounds of their
habitation; 27 that they should seek God, if haply they
might feel after him and find him, though he is not far
from each one of us: 28 for in him we live, and move, and
have our being; as certain even of your own poets have
said,*

For we are also his offspring.

*29 Being then the offspring of God, we ought not to think
that the Godhead is like unto gold, or silver, or stone,
graven by art and device of man. 30 The times of ignorance therefore God overlooked; but now he commandeth
men that they should all everywhere repent: 31 inasmuch
as he hath appointed a day in which he will judge the world
in righteousness by the man whom he hath ordained;
whereof he hath given assurance unto all men, in that he
hath raised him from the dead.*

*32 Now when they heard of the resurrection of the dead,
some mocked; but others said, We will hear thee concerning this yet again. 33 Thus Paul went out from among
them. 34 But certain men clave unto him, and believed:
among whom also was Dionysius the Areopagite, and a
woman named Damaris, and others with them.*

Athens was not only the intellectual but also the religious center of the ancient world; for it was the seat of
all the prevailing schools of philosophy, and every religion
is determined by certain essential underlying, philosophic
conceptions as to God, man, the world, mind, and matter.
In this story are represented all the elements which con-
stitute the so-called "religions" of the modern world, and
it suggests how these systems are to be approached and
how they can be met by the followers of Christ.

First of all, there was idolatry, the worship of images,
or of the spirit which is supposed to reside in images.
What stirred Paul was not the artistic beauty of the statues
and shrines and altars and temples, but what these works

of art were known to represent: "His spirit was provoked within him as he beheld the city full of idols." It was commonly said that there were "more gods in Athens than men." Paul was moved by the thought of all the ignorance and superstition and vice and immorality by which idolatry is inevitably accompanied.

The modern world is absolutely "full of idols." It is actually appalling to notice how large a proportion of the human race are this day bowing before gods which men have made. Even the majority of those who theoretically adhere to some one of the "ethnic faiths" are practically fetish worshipers; even countless "Christians" worship images, and others displace God by some other object of real devotion and affection.

Paul also encountered Jews, both in their places of worship and in the places of public resort. Orthodox Judaism is to be found in every region of the modern world, and practical Judaism is represented by additional millions who trust and worship one living and true God, but who deny the deity, the resurrection, and the atoning work of Christ.

Among the philosophers of Athens, Paul met representatives of two schools whose tenets mold the beliefs of many modern religious systems and cults. The "Epicureans" were practically materialists and atheists. They taught that the real aim of existence is pleasure; that pleasure is the only good, and pain is the only evil; that virtue is to be sought only because it yields the most enjoyment; that man should free himself from all belief in the gods or in the immortality of the soul; that the universe was not created but resulted from a chance "concourse of atoms"; that since there is no future life and no judgment, "let us eat and drink, for to-morrow we die." It would be startling to discover how many men in all lands have adopted practically, many even unconsciously, exactly such a creed.

Then, too, there were the "Stoics." They had many admirable qualities, but their belief was in substance the same as modern "pantheism." For them, God was everything and everything was God; he was "the soul of the universe," but not distinct from it; the difference between sin and virtue, and the distinction between the human and the divine, ceased to exist. They taught men resignation and the conquest of circumstances; but they were fatalists and considered absolute apathy the highest moral attainment. It would be illuminating to learn how far Hinduism is pantheistic, how far Mohammedanism is fatalistic, and how far certain popular religious "fads" of America and England practically deny the personality of God, and identify the human and the divine.

To such philosophers the simplest Christian truths are absurd; Paul was regarded as a "babbler," a man who had "small scraps" of truth but such as could not be wrought into any world system. They could not even understand his language when he spoke of Jesus and the resurrection. Moved by sheer curiosity, and with supreme contempt, they allowed Paul to address them.

Paul begins his address with extreme courtesy, complimenting the Greeks upon the fact that they were "very religious"; he finds this illustrated by an altar which was dedicated "To AN UNKNOWN GOD." Playing upon the meaning of this dedication, he insists that, with all their wisdom and "religion," they do not know the true God. This God, Paul proceeds to describe for them; and he does so in such terms as to show the fundamental fallacies of all their systems of belief. False views of God are the essential errors of all the present "world religions"; a right view of God is absolutely essential to Christian faith. It is useless to attempt to reconcile the gospel with pantheism or materialism or naturalism.

Speaking of God in his relation to the world and to men, Paul declares God to be the Creator and the moral Governor of all truths which strike at the very heart of materialism, of pantheism, of polytheism, of atheism, of fetishism, and of idolatry. As to man, Paul proceeds to teach that he is the offspring of God, of one blood, accountable to God and under his providential care; this fact he establishes by a quotation from one of the Greek poets, either Aratus, or Cleanthes. As to sin, Paul treats it as offense against a personal Judge who now demands repentance in view of a new revelation which he has made for the guidance of man. As to the way of salvation, it is through Christ who is the appointed Judge whose real nature is proved by the fact of his resurrection from the dead.

Of course Luke has given us only the briefest outline of this matchless message, but even this precious fragment contains a definite reference to every essential part of the Christian faith. It must be carefully pondered by all who would understand the world religions and who would be prepared to meet them with courtesy and power in presenting the truth as it is in Christ Jesus.

The results of the address are said to have been meager, and on this ground Paul has been criticized for having been too philosophic. As a matter of fact, one of the judges was converted, also a woman of social prominence, "and others with them." If there was any "failure" it must be attributed to the intellectual pride of his hearers. Paul had been preaching in a university city.

5. PAUL AT CORINTH   Ch. 18:1-22

1 After these things he departed from Athens, and came to Corinth. 2 And he found a certain Jew named Aquila, a man of Pontus by race, lately come from Italy, with his wife Priscilla, because Claudius had commanded all the Jews to depart from Rome: and he came unto them; 3 and because he was of the same trade, he abode with them, and they wrought; for by their trade they were tentmakers. 4 And he reasoned in the synagogue every sabbath, and persuaded Jews and Greeks.

5 But when Silas and Timothy came down from Macedonia, Paul was constrained by the word, testifying to the Jews that Jesus was the Christ. 6 And when they opposed themselves and blasphemed, he shook out his raiment and said unto them, Your blood be upon your own heads; I am clean: from henceforth I will go unto the Gentiles. 7 And he departed thence, and went into the house of a certain man named Titus Justus, one that worshipped God, whose house joined hard to the synagogue. 8 And Crispus, the ruler of the synagogue, believed in the Lord with all his house; and many of the Corinthians hearing believed, and were baptized. 9 And the Lord said unto Paul in the night by a vision, Be not afraid, but speak and hold not thy peace: 10 for I am with thee, and no man shall set on thee to harm thee: for I have much people in this city. 11 And he dwelt there a year and six months, teaching the word of God among them. 12 But when Gallio was proconsul of Achaia, the Jews with one accord rose up against Paul and brought him before the judgment-seat, 13 saying, This man persuadeth men to worship God contrary to the law. 14 But when Paul was about to open his mouth, Gallio said unto the Jews, If indeed it were a matter of wrong or of wicked villany, O ye Jews, reason would that I should bear with you: 15 but if they are questions about words and names and your own law, look to it yourselves; I am not minded to be a judge of these matters. 16 And he drove them from the judgment-seat. 17 And they all laid hold on Sosthenes, the ruler of the synagogue, and beat him before the judgment-seat. And Gallio cared for none of these things.

18 And Paul, having tarried after this yet many days, took his leave of the brethren, and sailed thence for Syria, and with him Priscilla and Aquila: having shorn his head in Cenchreæ; for he had a vow. 19 And they came to Ephesus, and he left them there: but he himself entered into the synagogue, and reasoned with the Jews. 20 And when they asked him to abide a longer time, he consented not; 21 but taking his leave of them, and saying, I will return again unto you if God will, he set sail from Ephesus.

22 And when he had landed at Cæsarea, he went up and saluted the church, and went down to Antioch.

The experience through which Paul passed at Corinth was so serious and unusual that it is regarded as constituting a distinct crisis in his life. The causes of his discouragement were such as are common to Christians, particularly to workers on the foreign field. It may be helpful to enumerate these, and also the divine providences by which he was given relief; for thus some may find encouragement and help in hours of darkness.

First of all, Paul felt his loneliness; he looked eagerly for the arrival of Silas and Timothy, but meanwhile in the great heathen city there was no friend to whom he could go for companionship and sympathy. How often has a missionary of the cross felt weighed down in the midst of heathenism by the sense of isolation and separation from friends!

Then, too, Paul was embarrassed by lack of funds; he was compelled to resort to his trade as a tentmaker to secure means of livelihood. This was not always the case. Paul was not an artisan; he was usually a traveler, preacher, scholar, supported by family and friends. He was not ashamed to work with his hands; still, financial need is always depressing, and particularly when one sees that his Christian work is suffering for lack of more liberal support.

Furthermore, the antagonism of the Jews was especially bitter; "they opposed themselves and blasphemed"; yet these were his own countrymen, whom he dearly loved, for whom he would have given his life, from whom he might have expected sympathy and support. Many Christian workers find no encouragement in the home circle; many missionaries find their greatest obstacle in the lives of nominal Christians on the foreign field.

Possibly the chief cause of depression was the character of the city in which he was attempting to work. It was the capital of the province of Achaia, rich, prosperous, intellectual, but its moral corruption was so deep and universal as to be proverbial throughout the Roman world; it shocked even the pagan sense of decency. Commercialism and materialism were absolutely absorbing; and the intellectual pride was almost invincible. Are followers of

Christ never disheartened by prevailing conditions? Do missionaries never feel depressed by the dead weight of heathen corruption and moral degradation?

The means of relief afforded the apostle have likewise many parallels in the experiences of modern life. First, he formed new friendships; henceforth Aquila and Priscilla held a large place in his life. "Old friends are the best," but new ones must be found or the circle will grow distressingly small.

The daily routine of tentmaking was in itself a providential relief from anxiety and distress of mind; the obvious tasks of daily life, which seem simple and necessary, help to cheer and strengthen the worker.

The preaching on the Sabbath days was a source of great satisfaction to the apostle; however lonely one may be, there is always a deep joy in testifying for Christ.

The arrival of Silas and Timothy with gifts from Macedonia tells the story of the encouragement which comes from reunion with precious friends. The supreme cause of relief, however, was found in a new vision of Christ. By it Paul was assured of the presence, the power, and the saving purpose of his Lord. Thus strengthened, Paul achieved the task of founding at Corinth a strong Christian church. From Corinth, also he wrote letters of great comfort to the Thessalonian church. The place of discouragement often becomes the scene of glorious victory.

Shortly after the vision was granted to Paul, he was given an example of the protection then promised him by the Lord. This incident has been interpreted in two quite opposite ways. The Jews united to drag Paul before Gallio, the newly appointed governor of Achaia, hoping to have the apostle expelled from the city; but Gallio refused to entertain their charge, which specified no crime or misdemeanor, but involved merely a question of Jewish law, and he drove the Jews from his judgment seat. The Greeks gladly seized the opportunity to administer a beating to Sosthenes, the leader of the Jewish mob. Gentiles have always enjoyed this form of amusement. "And Gallio cared for none of these things," therefore Gallio has been taken as a type of religious indifference. This, however, is not the point. Gallio was not irreligious, according to his own knowledge and light. "Sweet Gallio" as he was called, the brother of Seneca, the famous philosopher, was a man of most genial and attractive character; and here he stands forth as one who vindicated the majesty of the law and of justice; he insisted that no man should be tried as a criminal because of his religious beliefs. Gallio is really a noble example of religious tolerance.

By a few swift strokes Luke now traces the course of Paul as he completed his work in Corinth, and journeyed by way of Ephesus to Caesarea and Jerusalem and Antioch. Two or three touches are significant as links to the narratives which follow. The vow taken by Paul and his eagerness to celebrate "the feast" in Jerusalem indicate how truly he could claim ever to have observed the traditions of the Jews. The removal of Priscilla and Aquila to Ephesus and the favorable impression produced by Paul himself in his brief visit prepare the way for the long stay which Paul made in that important city when on his third missionary journey.

D. PAUL'S THIRD MISSIONARY JOURNEY
Chs. 18:23 to 21:16

1. APOLLOS AND THE DISCIPLES OF JOHN THE BAPTIST   Chs. 18:23 to 19:7

23 And having spent some time there, he departed, and went through the region of Galatia, and Phrygia, in order, establishing all the disciples.

24 Now a certain Jew named Apollos, an Alexandrian by race, an eloquent man, came to Ephesus; and he was mighty in the scriptures. 25 This man had been instructed in the way of the Lord; and being fervent in spirit, he spake and taught accurately the things concerning Jesus, knowing only the baptism of John: 26 and he began to speak boldly in the synagogue. But when Priscilla and Aquila heard him, they took him unto them, and expounded unto him the way of God more accurately. 27 And when he was minded to pass over into Achaia, the brethren encouraged him, and wrote to the disciples to receive him: and when he was come, he helped them much that had believed through grace; 28 for he powerfully confuted the Jews, and that publicly, showing by the scriptures that Jesus was the Christ.

1 And it came to pass, that, while Apollos was at Corinth, Paul having passed through the upper country came to Ephesus, and found certain disciples: 2 and he said unto them, Did ye receive the Holy Spirit when ye believed? And they said unto him, Nay, we did not so much as hear whether the Holy Spirit was given. 3 And he said, Into what then were ye baptized? And they said, Into John's baptism. 4 And Paul said, John baptized with the baptism of repentance, saying unto the people that they should believe on him that should come after him, that is, on Jesus. 5 And when they heard this, they were baptized into the name of the Lord Jesus. 6 And when Paul had laid his hands upon them, the Holy Spirit came on them; and they spake with tongues, and prophesied. 7 And they were in all about twelve men.

The main feature of what is known as Paul's third missionary journey was his stay of nearly three years in the city of Ephesus. The record of this long residence is introduced by the mention of two incidents which occurred, one before and the other just after his arrival; both prepare the reader for the account of the fruitful service of the three years by emphasizing anew the full gospel which Paul proclaimed and the presence of the Holy Spirit by whose power the work was done.

The first incident introduces Apollos, one of the great characters of the early church. He was born in Alexandria, the center of the broadest culture of the day; he was a man of great eloquence and fervor, a Jew who was carefully instructed in the Old Testament Scriptures, a believer in Jesus who knew of his life and teachings; but he was a disciple of John the Baptist and was ignorant of the death, resurrection, and ascension of Christ, and of the Pentecostal gift of the Holy Spirit. He must have been a humble-minded and noble soul, for after bold and impressive public teaching he allowed two poor tentmakers to show him his ignorance and to tell him the full truth concerning Christ; these two disciples were Priscilla and Aquila, and the woman is mentioned first, as the one who probably had the leading part in showing the great preacher his ignorance of the truth. It would not have been easy for Apollos to continue his work in Ephesus; but provided with letters of commendation from the Ephesian Christians, he crossed to Corinth and became a mighty power in proclaiming the grace of God in Christ Jesus.

The book of The Acts contains few more striking lessons for the preachers of today. Many good, gifted, eloquent, earnest men know or declare only "the baptism of John"; they call men to repent of sins, they insist on social justice and public integrity, and they emphasize the teachings and the example of Jesus, but they are silent as to the absolute necessity of a new birth by the power of the Holy Spirit. Ethics and social reform are absolutely essential parts of the gospel message, but they must not supplant and can only follow the proclamation of a living and divine Christ, through faith in whom alone men receive in all fullness the gift of his Spirit.

This story of Apollos prepares us for the strange experience which awaited Paul on his arrival in Ephesus. Apollos had gone, but the apostle at once encountered twelve other disciples of John the Baptist. They were introduced to Paul as "disciples," but the apostle was bewildered because they had none of the gifts of the Spirit; he asked them whether they had received the Holy Spirit when they believed; for of course every Christian believer has the unfailing presence and power of the Holy Spirit.

They replied that they knew nothing of such a gift of the Spirit as Paul implied. He then asked who they were; who could they be? They declared that they were followers of John the Baptist. Then Paul understood their defect; he told them about Jesus, of his death and resurrection and present power; and when they had heard about Jesus they believed in Jesus, they were baptized in his name and were filled with his Spirit, and they were granted the gifts of "tongues" and of prophecy.

There are men like Apollos in Christian pulpits, but there are many more like these twelve "disciples" in the pews of Christian churches. They are sincere men, they hate their sins, they believe in the teachings of Jesus, they admire the Sermon on the Mount, they yearn for the highest and best things, but they lack spiritual power. Why? Because they are "disciples of John," they have not fixed their hearts and their hopes upon a divine, risen, glorified Christ, they do not know "the grace of God." When, however, they learn the full gospel and yield themselves to Christ, they are not merely baptized with water, but also by the Holy Spirit.

2. THE WORK OF PAUL IN EPHESUS   Ch. 19:8-41

8 And he entered into the synagogue, and spake boldly for the space of three months, reasoning and persuading as to the things concerning the kingdom of God. 9 But when some were hardened and disobedient, speaking evil of the Way before the multitude, he departed from them, and separated the disciples, reasoning daily in the school of Tyrannus. 10 And this continued for the space of two years; so that all they that dwelt in Asia heard the word of the Lord, both Jews and Greeks. 11 And God wrought special miracles by the hands of Paul: 12 insomuch that unto the sick were carried away from his body handkerchiefs or aprons, and the diseases departed from them, and the evil spirits went out. 13 But certain also of the strolling Jews, exorcists, took upon them to name over them that had the evil spirits the name of the Lord Jesus, saying, I adjure you by Jesus whom Paul preacheth. 14 And there were seven sons of one Sceva, a Jew, a chief priest, who did this. 15 And the evil spirit answered and said unto them, Jesus I know, and Paul I know; but who are ye? 16 And the man in whom the evil spirit was leaped on them, and mastered both of them, and prevailed against them, so that they fled out of that house naked and wounded. 17 And this became known to all, both Jews and Greeks, that dwelt at Ephesus; and fear fell upon them all, and the name of the Lord Jesus was magnified. 18 Many also of them that had believed came, confessing, and declaring their deeds. 19 And not a few of them that practised magical arts brought their books together and burned them in the sight of all; and they counted the price of them, and found it fifty thousand pieces of silver. 20 So mightily grew the word of the Lord and prevailed.

21 Now after these things were ended, Paul purposed in the spirit, when he had passed through Macedonia and Achaia, to go to Jerusalem, saying, After I have been there, I must also see Rome. 22 And having sent into Macedonia two of them that ministered unto him, Timothy and Erastus, he himself stayed in Asia for a while.

23 And about that time there arose no small stir concerning the Way. 24 For a certain man named Demetrius, a silversmith, who made silver shrines of Diana, brought no little business unto the craftsmen; 25 whom he gathered together, with the workmen of like occupation, and said, Sirs, ye know that by this business we have our wealth. 26 And ye see and hear, that not alone at Ephesus, but almost throughout all Asia, this Paul hath persuaded and turned away much people, saying that they are no gods, that are made with hands: 27 and not only is there danger that this our trade come into disrepute; but also that the temple of the great goddess Diana be made of no account, and that she should even be deposed from her magnificence whom all Asia and the world worshippeth. 28 And when they heard this they were filled with wrath, and cried out, saying, Great is Diana of the Ephesians. 29 And the city was filled with the confusion: and they rushed with one accord into the theatre, having

seized Gaius and Aristarchus, men of Macedonia, Paul's companions in travel. 30 And when Paul was minded to enter in unto the people, the disciples suffered him not. 31 And certain also of the Asiarchs, being his friends, sent unto him and besought him not to adventure himself into the theatre. 32 Some therefore cried one thing, and some another: for the assembly was in confusion; and the more part knew not wherefore they were come together. 33 And they brought Alexander out of the multitude, the Jews putting him forward. And Alexander beckoned with the hand, and would have made a defence unto the people. 34 But when they perceived that he was a Jew, all with one voice about the space of two hours cried out, Great is Diana of the Ephesians. 35 And when the townclerk had quieted the multitude, he saith, Ye men of Ephesus, what man is there who knoweth not that the city of the Ephesians is temple-keeper of the great Diana, and of the image which fell down from Jupiter? 36 Seeing then that these things cannot be gainsaid, ye ought to be quiet, and to do nothing rash. 37 For ye have brought hither these men, who are neither robbers of temples nor blasphemers of our goddess. 38 If therefore Demetrius, and the craftsmen that are with him, have a matter against any man, the courts are open, and there are proconsuls: let them accuse one another. 39 But if ye seek anything about other matters, it shall be settled in the regular assembly. 40 For indeed we are in danger to be accused concerning this day's riot, there being no cause for it: and as touching it we shall not be able to give account of this concourse. 41 And when he had thus spoken, he dismissed the assembly.

The gift of the Holy Spirit to the twelve disciples of John, when they became believers in Jesus, has sometimes been called the "Ephesian Pentecost." Possibly that term might be applied to the further account of the experience of Paul in the great heathen city; for like the story of Pentecost it is a narrative not only of the gift of tongues, but of bold testimony, of multitudes converted, of lives transformed by the power of the Holy Spirit. The historian gives few details, and summarizes the events of three years in a few brief paragraphs.

As was frequently the case, the apostle preached first to the Jews and then turned to the Gentiles, using as his auditorium the schoolroom of Tyrannus. As a result of his testimony the whole province of Asia was evangelized. Additional impressiveness was given to the preaching of Paul by the extraordinary miracles which he worked in the name of Jesus. When certain traveling exorcists attempted to use this sacred name to expel a demon, the man possessed leaped on them and drove them from the house "naked and wounded." When this was known in the city the results were startling: great "fear fell upon them all, and the name of the Lord Jesus was magnified"; further, many believers confessed their secret sins; most significant of all, those who practiced magic arts acknowledged their fraud, and made a bonfire of parchments on which their incantations and formulas were written, and so sacrificed what would have amounted in value to more than eight thousand dollars.

It is not strange that such success at Ephesus filled Paul with an eager desire for even wider fields of labor and that he lifted his eyes toward Rome; it was necessary, however, for him first to revisit the churches established on his former missionary journey, and to take from them a contribution to the poor saints at Jerusalem; but henceforth the story of The Acts is chiefly concerned with the steps by which Paul was brought providentially to the Imperial City, the capital of the world.

One incident, however, is related at the close of the experiences in Ephesus; it is dramatic, even ludicrous in some respects; but it forms a climax to the story of Paul's success, for it shows how the forces of the enemy were terrified, baffled, defeated. The very institution of idolatry is seen to have been tottering and that, too, in its chief seat and center.

Demetrius, a silversmith, a man of evident influence in the city, summons his fellow craftsmen and reminds them that so many people are turning from idol worship that the sale of images and of models of the great temple of Diana has almost ceased. Like many other men in similar circumstances he tries to veil his covetousness beneath a show of great religious zeal and of love for their goddess. A mob is quickly aroused; the whole city is stirred; two companions of Paul are seized; the crowds surge to the public theater; Paul is prevented by his friends from venturing thither, where he certainly would have been killed. When a Jew, Alexander by name, is put forward to deliver an address, possibly to explain that the Jews were not at fault, the mob shows its real temper, its unwillingness to listen to any defense, and for two hours the people rend the air with the mad cry: "Great is Diana of the Ephesians." At this crisis the town clerk comes forward with a speech of amusing shrewdness and force. He tells the crowd that they are shouting to prove a fact which no one has denied; further he insists that Paul and his companions have been guilty of no crime, and that if Demetrius and his friends have any grievance the law courts are open and there, not at the hands of a mob, justice will be administered; lastly he reminds the people that such disorders endanger the liberties allowed to the city by Rome, and that someone will be called to account before the imperial government for such a riotous assembly. These wise words prevail, and the speaker dismisses the assembly. Such an incident demonstrates the defeat of heathenism and the increasing triumph of the cause of Christ.

3. PAUL'S VISIT TO GREECE AND HIS RETURN TO MILETUS Ch. 20:1-16

1 And after the uproar ceased, Paul having sent for the disciples and exhorted them, took leave of them, and departed to go into Macedonia. 2 And when he had gone through those parts, and had given them much exhortation, he came into Greece. 3 And when he had spent three months there, and a plot was laid against him by the Jews as he was about to set sail for Syria, he determined to return through Macedonia. 4 And there accompanied him as far as Asia, Sopater of Berœa, the son of Pyrrhus; and of the Thessalonians, Aristarchus and Secundus; and Gaius of Derbe, and Timothy; and of Asia, Tychicus and Trophimus. 5 But these had gone before, and were waiting for us at Troas. 6 And we sailed away from Philippi after the days of unleavened bread, and came unto them to Troas in five days; where we tarried seven days.

7 And upon the first day of the week, when we were gathered together to break bread, Paul discoursed with them, intending to depart on the morrow; and prolonged his speech until midnight. 8 And there were many lights in the upper chamber where we were gathered together. 9 And there sat in the window a certain young man named Eutychus, borne down with deep sleep; and as Paul discoursed yet longer, being borne down by his sleep he fell down from the third story, and was taken up dead. 10 And Paul went down, and fell on him, and embracing him said, Make ye no ado; for his life is in him. 11 And when he was gone up, and had broken the bread, and eaten, and had talked with them a long while, even till break of day, so he departed. 12 And they brought the lad alive, and were not a little comforted.

13 But we, going before to the ship, set sail for Assos, there intending to take in Paul: for so had he appointed, intending himself to go by land. 14 And when he met us at Assos, we took him in, and came to Mitylene. 15 And sailing from thence, we came the following day over against Chios; and the next day we touched at Samos; and the day after we came to Miletus. 16 For Paul had determined to sail past Ephesus, that he might not have to spend time in Asia; for he was hastening, if it were possible for him, to be at Jerusalem the day of Pentecost.

With surprising brevity Luke sketches the journey of Paul to Macedonia and Achaia. The Second Epistle of Paul to the Corinthians throws a clear light upon the purpose of the apostle and upon the trials through which he was passing. This letter was written in Macedonia on his way to Greece. While in Ephesus he had addressed a letter to the Galatians and at least one to the Christians of Corinth. On reaching the latter city, he wrote his famous letter to the believers in Rome. Toward that city his thought and heart were turning constantly, and Luke seems almost impatient to bring his readers to Jerusalem and to the events which enabled the apostle finally to realize his hopes. One touch here given is significant; Luke mentions a plot of the Jews which prevented Paul from making the rapid sea voyage to Syria and compelled him tediously to retrace his steps through Macedonia. This Jewish malice, continually appearing, awaits the apostle in Jerusalem; there it will appear in its most malignant form, but it will be an instrument in the hands of Providence to bring the apostle as a witness for Christ to Caesar's palace.

As Paul started northward through Macedonia, it is evident that, in addition to the traveling companions already named, Luke joined the company; for now the compressed narrative becomes a story of minute incident; it is written in the first person and is evidently the work of an eyewitness. Between Philippi and Miletus the one important event is in connection with the stay of Paul at Troas. There he tarried a week, and there he performed his most notable miracle. He met with the disciples to celebrate the Lord's Supper, and to speak to them words of cheer. Eutychus fell from the window and was killed, but Paul restored him to life. The presence of such divine power was comforting to the believers, and undoubtedly encouraging to Paul as he moved rapidly forward to meet the supreme trials of his life.

4. PAUL'S ADDRESS TO THE EPHESIAN ELDERS
Ch. 20:17-38

17 And from Miletus he sent to Ephesus, and called to him the elders of the church. 18 And when they were

come to him, he said unto them,

Ye yourselves know, from the first day that I set foot in Asia, after what manner I was with you all the time, 19 serving the Lord with all lowliness of mind, and with tears, and with trials which befell me by the plots of the Jews; 20 how I shrank not from declaring unto you anything that was profitable, and teaching you publicly, and from house to house, 21 testifying both to Jews and to Greeks repentance toward God, and faith toward our Lord Jesus Christ. 22 And now, behold, I go bound in the spirit unto Jerusalem, not knowing the things that shall befall me there: 23 save that the Holy Spirit testifieth unto me in every city, saying that bonds and afflictions abide me. 24 But I hold not my life of any account as dear unto myself, so that I may accomplish my course, and the ministry which I received from the Lord Jesus, to testify the gospel of the grace of God. 25 And now, behold, I know that ye all, among whom I went about preaching the kingdom, shall see my face no more. 26 Wherefore I testify unto you this day, that I am pure from the blood of all men. 27 For I shrank not from declaring unto you the whole counsel of God. 28 Take heed unto yourselves, and to all the flock, in which the Holy Spirit hath made you bishops, to feed the church of the Lord which he purchased with his own blood. 29 I know that after my departing grievous wolves shall enter in among you, not sparing the flock; 30 and from among your own selves shall men arise, speaking perverse things, to draw away the disciples after them. 31 Wherefore watch ye, remembering that by the space of three years I ceased not to admonish every one night and day with tears. 32 And now I commend you to God, and to the word of his grace, which is able to build you up, and to give you the inheritance among all them that are sanctified. 33 I coveted no man's silver, or gold, or apparel. 34 Ye yourselves know that these hands ministered unto my necessities, and to them that were with me. 35 In all things I gave you an example, that so laboring ye ought to help the weak, and to remember the words of the Lord Jesus, that he himself said, It is more blessed to give than to receive.

36 And when he had thus spoken, he kneeled down and

*prayed with them all. 37 And they all wept sore, and fell
on Paul's neck and kissed him, 38 sorrowing most of all
for the word which he had spoken, that they should behold his face no more. And they brought him on his way
unto the ship.*

The farewell address of Paul to the Ephesian elders,
more than any other passage of The Acts, reveals the
heart of the great apostle, his tenderness, his sympathy, his
affection, and his tears. No other paragraph contains
more direct and practical advice for Christian ministers
and missionaries; furthermore, its guidance and inspiration are such as to aid every follower of Christ in the conduct of life and in the fulfillment of duty.

In his journey toward Jerusalem, Paul could not spare
the time to visit Ephesus; he therefore summoned the
"elders," or "presbyters," of the church to meet him at
Miletus, thirty-six miles distant from the great heathen
city in which for three years he had worked with such
notable success. His purpose was not merely to enjoy the
privilege of meeting friends who had become dear to him
as fellow workers, but chiefly to encourage them to be
faithful in their care of the church which he was leaving
to their guidance and direction. So he reviewed the events
of the three past precious years he had spent among them,
and then told them of his present experiences and of his
fear that they should see his face "no more."

Looking backward (ch. 20:19-21), he reminds them
of his "lowliness of mind," his patience under trials, and
his faithfulness shown in teaching the whole gospel to all
classes and in all places, public and private. The essence
of that gospel message consisted in "repentance toward
God, and faith toward our Lord Jesus Christ" (v. 21).

As for the present, Paul declares that he is convinced
that it is his duty to press on to Jerusalem, although he is
aware of the bonds and afflictions which await him there;
and in this connection he expresses a courage which is
sublime. "I hold not my life of any account as dear unto

myself, so that I may accomplish my course, and the ministry which I received from the Lord Jesus, to testify the gospel of the grace of God."

Looking to the future, Paul is certain that his work in the Ephesian church is ended, and he exhorts the "elders" to be as faithful in their care of the flock as he has been. It is a sacred trust, for the church has been purchased with the precious blood of Christ. Vigilance will be necessary, for false teachers are certain to attack the church, like "grievous wolves." The elders must trust in God and depend upon his gracious word which can build them up and give them an inheritance among the saints. Lastly, Paul appeals to the supreme motive of unselfish love, and gives the example of his own life in Ephesus, where he labored with his own hands to support himself and to make it possible for him to continue his proclamation of the gospel; but he further urges such sacrificial service by quoting words of our Lord Jesus which are nowhere else recorded: "It is more blessed to give than to receive." Those followers of Christ who can reveal the virtues which Paul exhibited and encouraged will surely share some of the success which was granted the apostle at Ephesus, and will receive something of the affection which his fellow workers showed as they "fell on Paul's neck and kissed him," and "brought him on his way unto the ship."

5. PAUL AT TYRE AND CAESAREA   Ch. 21:1-16

1 And when it came to pass that we were parted from them and had set sail, we came with a straight course unto Cos, and the next day unto Rhodes, and from thence unto Patara: 2 and having found a ship crossing over unto Phœnicia, we went aboard, and set sail. 3 And when we had come in sight of Cyprus, leaving it on the left hand, we sailed unto Syria, and landed at Tyre; for there the ship was to unlade her burden. 4 And having found the disciples, we tarried there seven days: and these said to Paul through the Spirit, that he should not set foot in Jeru-

salem. 5 And when it came to pass that we had accomplished the days, we departed and went on our journey; and they all, with wives and children, brought us on our way till we were out of the city: and kneeling down on the beach, we prayed, and bade each other farewell; 6 and we went on board the ship, but they returned home again.

7 And when we had finished the voyage from Tyre, we arrived at Ptolemais; and we saluted the brethren, and abode with them one day. 8 And on the morrow we departed, and came unto Cæsarea: and entering into the house of Philip the evangelist, who was one of the seven, we abode with him. 9 Now this man had four virgin daughters, who prophesied. 10 And as we tarried there some days, there came down from Judæa a certain prophet, named Agabus. 11 And coming to us, and taking Paul's girdle, he bound his own feet and hands, and said, Thus saith the Holy Spirit, So shall the Jews at Jerusalem bind the man that owneth this girdle, and shall deliver him into the hands of the Gentiles. 12 And when we heard these things, both we and they of that place besought him not to go up to Jerusalem. 13 Then Paul answered, What do ye, weeping and breaking my heart? for I am ready not to be bound only, but also to die at Jerusalem for the name of the Lord Jesus. 14 And when he would not be persuaded, we ceased, saying, The will of the Lord be done.

15 And after these days we took up our baggage and went up to Jerusalem. 16 And there went with us also certain of the disciples from Cæsarea, bringing with them one Mnason of Cyprus, an early disciple, with whom we should lodge.

After leaving Miletus, Paul passed on to Tyre, to Ptolemais, and to Jerusalem. The brief story fixes the thought upon two great facts which prepare us for the closing scenes of The Acts: first, the deep affection in which Paul is held by his friends, and second, the matchless courage with which Paul faces the trials which are so certain and so near. These two factors enter into his experience at Tyre and Caesarea. In both places loving friends would detain him or turn him back from the path of duty; in

both places heroic bravery bears him forward to pain and
suffering, to bonds and imprisonment.

These facts explain the situation at Tyre, where the disciples "said to Paul through the Spirit, that he should not
set foot in Jerusalem." So some readers have concluded
that Paul disobeyed the Spirit, and in mere stubborn self-
will pushed on to the place of needless peril and suffered
the loss of liberty. The real meaning of the historian is
made quite clear when a similar experience, which came
to Paul in Caesarea, is narrated more in detail. There,
while Paul is entertained in the hospitable home of "Philip
the evangelist," a prophet, Agabus, arrives from Judea,
and by a striking symbol predicts Paul's approaching imprisonment. "Taking Paul's girdle, he bound his own
feet and hands, and said, Thus saith the Holy Spirit, So
shall the Jews at Jerusalem bind the man that owneth
this girdle, and shall deliver him into the hands of the
Gentiles. And when we heard these things, both we and
they of that place besought him not to go up to Jerusalem."
This is what had occurred at Tyre; that is, Paul had been
assured of his peril, and affectionate friends had attempted
to dissuade him from his purpose. This purpose, however,
was formed under the guidance of the Spirit. It was the
will of the Lord, as Paul well knew. For years he had
been preparing to bring to Jerusalem the collection for the
saints from the missionary churches of the west. It was
not stubborn self-confidence but heroic courage which led
Paul to reply: "What do ye, weeping and breaking my
heart? for I am ready not be bound only, but also to die
at Jerusalem for the name of the Lord Jesus." Agabus
did not rebuke the apostle, but united with Luke and the
other disciples in saying: "The will of the Lord be done."

According to "the will of the Lord," the way to Rome
lay through Jerusalem. He purposed that the Jews in
their national capital should have the opportunity of hearing the gospel from one who loved their nation, who had
come bearing gifts expressive of his devotion, one who

would speak before the chief council and give to the nation a final opportunity of accepting Jesus as the Messiah. It was the rejection of the message brought by Paul which sealed the fate of the nation and resulted in sending the gospel to Rome and the Gentile world.

E. PAUL'S IMPRISONMENT Chs. 21:17 to 26:32

1. THE ARREST Ch. 21:17-36

17 And when we were come to Jerusalem, the brethren received us gladly. 18 And the day following Paul went in with us unto James; and all the elders were present. 19 And when he had saluted them, he rehearsed one by one the things which God had wrought among the Gentiles through his ministry. 20 And they, when they heard it, glorified God; and they said unto him, Thou seest, brother, how many thousands there are among the Jews of them that have believed; and they are all zealous for the law: 21 and they have been informed concerning thee, that thou teachest all the Jews who are among the Gentiles to forsake Moses, telling them not to circumcise their children, neither to walk after the customs. 22 What is it therefore? they will certainly hear that thou art come. 23 Do therefore this that we say to thee: We have four men that have a vow on them; 24 these take, and purify thyself with them, and be at charges for them, that they may shave their heads: and all shall know that there is no truth in the things whereof they have been informed concerning thee; but that thou thyself also walkest orderly, keeping the law. 25 But as touching the Gentiles that have believed, we wrote, giving judgment that they should keep themselves from things sacrificed to idols, and from blood, and from what is strangled, and from fornication. 26 Then Paul took the men, and the next day purifying himself with them went into the temple, declaring the fulfilment of the days of purification, until the offering was offered for every one of them.

27 And when the seven days were almost completed, the Jews from Asia, when they saw him in the temple, stirred

*up all the multitude and laid hands on him, 28 crying out,
Men of Israel, help: This is the man that teacheth all men
everywhere against the people, and the law, and this place;
and moreover he brought Greeks also into the temple, and
hath defiled this holy place. 29 For they had before seen
with him in the city Trophimus the Ephesian, whom they
supposed that Paul had brought into the temple. 30 And
all the city was moved, and the people ran together; and
they laid hold on Paul, and dragged him out of the temple:
and straightway the doors were shut. 31 And as they were
seeking to kill him, tidings came up to the chief captain of
the band, that all Jerusalem was in confusion. 32 And
forthwith he took soldiers and centurions, and ran down
upon them: and they, when they saw the chief captain and
the soldiers, left off beating Paul. 33 Then the chief captain came near, and laid hold on him, and commanded
him to be bound with two chains; and inquired who he
was, and what he had done. 34 And some shouted one
thing, some another, among the crowd: and when he could
not know the certainty for the uproar, he commanded him
to be brought into the castle. 35 And when he came upon
the stairs, so it was that he was borne of the soldiers for
the violence of the crowd; 36 for the multitude of the
people followed after, crying out, Away with him.*

The remaining portion of The Acts is concerned wholly
with the experiences of Paul as a prisoner in the hands of
the Roman authorities; the period covered between the
time of his arrest in Jerusalem and his release in Rome is
reckoned at five years. The occasion of his arrest was an
endeavor he was making to remove a certain prejudice
against him felt by members of the church in Jerusalem.
He had been welcomed to the city by the Christian leaders
who rejoiced to learn of his success among the Gentiles.
These leaders, however, knew that many members of the
church in Jerusalem, which was composed wholly of converted Jews, believed the false report that Paul not only
admitted Gentiles to the church but compelled Jews who
accepted Christ to give up their national customs and to

forsake the law of Moses. To disprove the false reports, to bring perfect unity into the church, even to conciliate the mad hatred of the unbelieving Jews, Paul was advised to accept the Nazirite vow and to observe its exacting ritual. This advice Paul accepted; and as the ceremonials connected with this vow were quite elaborate and expensive, he also agreed to defray the charges for four poorer members of the local church. Thus he gave a public and certain proof that he was loyal to the Jewish race and its customs. Paul has been severely criticized for his action, which has been termed compromising and hypocritical; it has been regarded as the unnecessary cause of his arrest. This, however, is quite to miss the point of the story and to misunderstand the principles of Paul. He had rejected the law as a means of justification, not as a mode of life; he did not trust to its observance to secure his salvation, but he practiced its ceremonies as one who loved his nation and who was glad to avoid any needless offense to his fellow countrymen. Then as to his arrest, it was not due to his observance of the law, but to a wholly false charge that he had violated the law. Certain Jews from Asia raised a tumult by seizing Paul, gathering a crowd, and crying out that he had defiled the Temple by bringing Gentiles within its courts. The charge was wholly untrue. Paul was the victim of malicious falsehood, and the real intention of the writer, the true force of the narrative, is not to suggest any fault on the part of the apostle, but to emphasize the guilt of the Jews. They were endeavoring to have Paul put to death as an apostate and a blasphemer, yet they seized him at the very time and place where he was showing his intense love for the Temple and his loyalty to Jewish law and customs. The circumstances prove that his enemies were moved wholly by malice and envy, that their real enmity was against Christ, and that their violence to Paul was actually another rejection of the gospel.

Thus as the frenzied mob in the Temple seize and beat the apostle, as he is rescued by the Roman soldiers who were stationed in the neighboring castle of Antonia, charged with the preservation of order in the city, there is given a picture typical of the experiences of Paul during the next five or more years. He is a prisoner unjustly confined, but protected by Roman officers from the murderous hatred of the Jews. These experiences are symbolized by the scene thus drawn by Luke: "Then the chief captain came near, and laid hold on him, and commanded him to be bound with two chains; and . . . commanded him to be brought into the castle. And . . . the multitude of the people followed after, crying out, Away with him."

2. PAUL'S DEFENSE BEFORE THE JEWISH PEOPLE
Chs. 21:37 to 22:22

37 And as Paul was about to be brought into the castle, he saith unto the chief captain, May I say something unto thee? And he said, Dost thou know Greek? 38 Art thou not then the Egyptian, who before these days stirred up to sedition and led out into the wilderness the four thousand men of the Assassins? 39 But Paul said, I am a Jew, of Tarsus in Cilicia, a citizen of no mean city: and I beseech thee, give me leave to speak unto the people. 40 And when he had given him leave, Paul, standing on the stairs, beckoned with the hand unto the people; and when there was made a great silence, he spake unto them in the Hebrew language, saying,

1 Brethren and fathers, hear ye the defence which I now make unto you.

2 And when they heard that he spake unto them in the Hebrew language, they were the more quiet: and he saith,

3 I am a Jew, born in Tarsus of Cilicia, but brought up in this city, at the feet of Gamaliel, instructed according to the strict manner of the law of our fathers, being zealous for God, even as ye all are this day: 4 and I persecuted this Way unto the death, binding and delivering into prisons both men and women. 5 As also the high priest doth bear me witness, and all the estate of the elders: from whom also I received letters unto the brethren, and journeyed to Damascus to bring them also that were there unto Jerusalem

*in bonds to be punished. 6 And it came to pass, that, as
I made my journey, and drew nigh unto Damascus, about
noon, suddenly there shone from heaven a great light round
about me. 7 And I fell unto the ground, and heard a voice
saying unto me, Saul, Saul, why persecutest thou me? 8
And I answered, Who art thou, Lord? And he said unto
me, I am Jesus of Nazareth, whom thou persecutest. 9
And they that were with me beheld indeed the light, but
they heard not the voice of him that spake to me. 10 And
I said, What shall I do, Lord? And the Lord said unto me,
Arise, and go into Damascus; and there it shall be told thee
of all things which are appointed for thee to do. 11 And
when I could not see for the glory of that light, being led
by the hand of them that were with me I came into Damascus. 12 And one Ananias, a devout man according to the
law, well reported of by all the Jews that dwelt there, 13
came unto me, and standing by me said unto me, Brother
Saul, receive thy sight. And in that very hour I looked
up on him. 14 And he said, The God of our fathers hath
appointed thee to know his will, and to see the Righteous
One, and to hear a voice from his mouth. 15 For thou
shalt be a witness for him unto all men of what thou hast
seen and heard. 16 And now why tarriest thou? arise,
and be baptized, and wash away thy sins, calling on his
name. 17 And it came to pass, that, when I had returned
to Jerusalem, and while I prayed in the temple, I fell into
a trance, 18 and saw him saying unto me, Make haste, and
get thee quickly out of Jerusalem; because they will not receive of thee testimony concerning me. 19 And I said,
Lord, they themselves know that I imprisoned and beat in
every synagogue them that believed on thee: 20 and when
the blood of Stephen thy witness was shed, I also was
standing by, and consenting, and keeping the garments of
them that slew him. 21 And he said unto me, Depart:
for I will send thee forth far hence unto the Gentiles.*

*22 And they gave him audience unto this word; and
they lifted up their voice, and said, Away with such a fellow from the earth: for it is not fit that he should live.*

The Roman captain at whose order Paul was being
placed under arrest was greatly mistaken as to the char-

acter of his prisoner; he supposed him to be a notorious Egyptian outlaw, impostor, and desperado, who some time before had led an insurrection and had escaped when defeated. He was much surprised when Paul addressed him in Greek, with an accent which betokened a man of refinement and culture. He was still more surprised to learn that Paul was a citizen of Tarsus, a city which had been shown high favor by the Roman government. For this reason he was ready to grant Paul's request for the privilege of addressing the people, and the more so because he was moved by the hope that such an address might give information which would be useful to himself.

The defense which Paul delivers seems to be, at first, a mere recital of his own conversion, a story with which Luke has already made his readers familiar; but a more careful examination of the address shows that it is a skillful argument, so arranged as to prove that the course of Paul has been divinely ordered and thus to imply that those who oppose Paul are, in reality, placing themselves in opposition to God.

Three steps have been noticed in his reasoning.

a. By birth, education, and earlier experience Paul has been in perfect agreement with his hearers. He is a Jew, educated in Jerusalem at the feet of a famous rabbi, he has been so zealous for the law that he formerly persecuted all who accepted Jesus as the Way and were known to live as his followers. Therefore, if Paul now differs from other Jews it must be because of some supernatural influence which has come into his life.

b. The divine power which suddenly transformed Paul from a persecutor to an apostle had been manifested by a vision of Jesus, whom Paul, on his way to Damascus, saw living and glorified, and further by a miracle wrought upon him by a devout Jew named Ananias, at whose hands he received his lost sight, and before whom he confessed the faith which secured the forgiveness of his sins. Here Paul is incidentally but forcefully reminding his hearers that

Jesus of Nazareth is the true Savior, and that to persecute his followers is a grievous sin.

c. Paul states that his relation to the Gentiles, his work among them, and his message to them, are wholly due to a divine purpose, and have been occasioned by the unwillingness of the Jews to receive him, who, because of his previous course as a fanatical defender of the Jewish law, is the most credible of witnesses as he now testifies to the truth of beliefs he once so rejected and hated. This last statement raises the question, Will these Jews now act as did their fellow citizens of twenty years before? Will they reject the gospel, and if so can Paul be blamed if he turns again to preach this gospel to Gentiles?

These questions may have begun to press upon the minds of the hearers, but the very word "Gentiles" is too hateful for them to endure. They are too frenzied to yield to the calm, unanswerable argument of the apostle. "They lifted up their voice, and said, Away with such a fellow from the earth: for it is not fit that he should live." It is a fateful hour; in rejecting Paul, the people are again rejecting Christ; and one who rejects Christ is always self-condemned; he is truly "fighting against God."

3. Paul Before the Jewish Council
Chs. 22:23 to 23:11

23 And as they cried out, and threw off their garments, and cast dust into the air, 24 the chief captain commanded him to be brought into the castle, bidding that he should be examined by scourging, that he might know for what cause they so shouted against him. 25 And when they had tied him up with the thongs, Paul said unto the centurion that stood by, Is it lawful for you to scourge a man that is a Roman, and uncondemned? 26 And when the centurion heard it, he went to the chief captain and told him, saying, What art thou about to do? for this man is a Roman. 27 And the chief captain came and said unto him, Tell me, art thou a Roman? And he said, Yea. 28 And the chief captain answered, With a great sum obtained I this citizenship. And Paul said, But I am a Roman born. 29 They then that were about to examine him straightway departed from him: and the chief captain also was afraid when he knew that he was a Roman, and because he had bound him.

30 But on the morrow, desiring to know the certainty wherefore he was accused of the Jews, he loosed him, and commanded the chief priests and all the council to come together, and brought Paul down and set him before them.

1 And Paul, looking stedfastly on the council, said, Brethren, I have lived before God in all good conscience until this day. 2 And the high priest Ananias commanded them that stood by him to smite him on the mouth. 3 Then said Paul unto him, God shall smite thee, thou whited wall: and sittest thou to judge me according to the law, and commandest me to be smitten contrary to the law? 4 And they that stood by said, Revilest thou God's high priest? 5 And Paul said, I knew not, brethren, that he was high priest: for it is written, Thou shalt not speak evil of a ruler of thy people. 6 But when Paul perceived that the one part were Sadducees and the other Pharisees, he cried out in the council, Brethren, I am a Pharisee, a son of Pharisees: touching the hope and resurrection of the dead I am called in question. 7 And when he had so said, there arose a dissension between the Pharisees and Sadducees; and the assembly was divided. 8 For the Sadducees say that there is no resurrection, neither angel, nor spirit; but the Pharisees confess both. 9 And there arose a great clamor: and some of the scribes of the Pharisees' part stood up, and strove, saying, We find no evil in this man: and what if a spirit hath spoken to him, or an angel? 10 And when there arose a great dissension, the chief captain, fearing lest Paul should be torn in pieces by them, commanded the soldiers to go down and take him by force from among them, and bring him into the castle.

11 And the night following the Lord stood by him, and said, Be of good cheer: for as thou hast testified concerning me at Jerusalem, so must thou bear witness also at Rome.

The defense of Paul had failed to persuade the mob of angry Jews, but it likewise gave little light to the Roman captain. He could not follow its arguments; at least it gave no clue to the crime of which the Jews implied Paul was guilty. To learn the facts from the apostle he determined to have him examined by torture. The apostle was bound and about to be cruelly scourged, when he disclosed the fact that he was a Roman citizen, and therefore could not lawfully be bound, much less scourged, without a fair trial. The chief captain and his lieutenants were terrified at the disclosure; and Paul was at once treated with extreme courtesy.

The Roman officer, defeated in his design to learn why the Jews were so enraged at Paul, determined to place him on trial before the supreme Jewish council, the Sanhedrin. On the morning following, the council was summoned and Paul was arraigned before them. Little did the Roman soldiers dream that on that day, not the apostle, but his judges were to be tried and condemned. Christ was to be presented to the nation, in the person of its rulers; Christ was again to be rejected and the doom of the nation sealed.

As to Paul's conduct before the Sanhedrin two questions have been proposed: (a) Was Paul moved by anger when he rebuked the high priest? and (b) Was he attempting a shrewd subterfuge when he proposed the question of the "resurrection"?

As to the former, it seems best to conclude that Paul, in the crowded assembly, had not perceived that the speaker who commanded that he should be smitten on the mouth was the high priest. The reply of Paul was not an angry imprecation; it was a solemn warning or prophecy. These very judges, in their pretended zeal for the law of Moses, were really acting contrary to its spirit and demands. When Paul was informed of the actual rank of the speaker, his reply was courteous and he implied that he would not willingly be guilty of even an apparent breach of the courtesy due to one occupying a sacred office.

As to the "resurrection," Paul showed his true insight in declaring that the whole question of his guilt or innocence was involved in the acceptance or rejection of this one doctrine. The real charge against him was not that he was not loyal to Jewish law or Jewish beliefs; the real charge was that he preached the resurrection, and declared that the resurrection of Jesus is the proof that he is the Messiah. It was, after all, then, a question of resurrection that was before the council. Paul was well aware how the judges were divided upon this point; he knew the real unbelief of the Sadducees, and he must have felt a secret satisfaction in having them rebuked by their fellow judges for attempting to convict a man of renouncing the law which they so openly rejected. It was not mere worldly cunning which animated the apostle; he had declared before the council the essential doctrine of the Christian faith, for which he was on trial. His declaration produced a tumult in the court. The Sadducees would have torn Paul to pieces; the Pharisees would have protected him from violence, as they admitted that he was guilty of no crime and at most was only the victim of some hallucination, if not the recipient of some divine message. Paul would have been killed had not the chief captain rescued him and carried him away to the castle.

That night Paul was comforted by a new vision of his Lord. There was a distinct divine approval of Paul's course; there was new assurance of supernatural aid and protection. Paul was promised that the wish of his life was to be realized. He was to testify for Christ in Rome; but by what strange providences this was to be brought to pass, Paul could not have dreamed.

4. PAUL SENT TO CAESAREA   Ch. 23:12-35

12 And when it was day, the Jews banded together, and bound themselves under a curse, saying that they would neither eat nor drink till they had killed Paul. 13 And they were more than forty that made this conspiracy. 14 And they came to the chief priests and the elders, and said, We have bound ourselves under a great curse, to taste nothing until we have killed Paul. 15 Now therefore do ye with the council signify to the chief captain that he bring him down unto you, as though ye would judge of his case more exactly: and we, before he comes near, are ready to slay him. 16 But Paul's sister's son heard of their lying in wait, and he came and entered into the castle and told Paul. 17 And Paul called unto him one of the centurions, and said, Bring this young man unto the chief captain; for he hath something to tell him. 18 So he took him, and brought him to the chief captain, and saith, Paul the prisoner called me unto him, and asked me to bring this young man unto thee, who hath something to say to thee. 19 And the chief captain took him by the hand, and going aside asked him privately, What is it that thou hast to tell me? 20 And he said, The Jews have agreed to ask thee to bring down Paul to-morrow unto the council, as though thou wouldest inquire somewhat more exactly concerning him. 21 Do not thou therefore yield unto them: for there lie in wait for him of them more than forty men, who have bound themselves under a curse, neither to eat nor to drink till they have slain him: and now are they ready, looking for the promise from thee. 22 So the chief captain let the young man go, charging him, Tell no man that thou hast signified these things to me. 23 And he called unto him two of the centurions, and said, Make ready two hundred soldiers to go as far as Cæsarea, and horsemen threescore and ten, and spearmen two hundred, at the third hour of the night: 24 and he bade them *provide beasts, that they might set Paul thereon, and bring him safe unto Felix the governor. 25 And he wrote a letter after this form:*

26 Claudius Lysias unto the most excellent governor Felix, greeting. 27 This man was seized by the Jews, and was about to be slain of them, when I came upon them with the soldiers and rescued him, having learned that he was a Roman. 28 And desiring to know the cause wherefore they accused him, I brought him down unto their council: 29 whom I found to be accused about questions of their law, but to have nothing laid to his charge worthy of death or of bonds. 30 And when it was shown to me that there would be a plot against the man, I sent him to thee forth-

*with, charging his accusers also to speak against him be-
fore thee.*

*31 So the soldiers, as it was commanded them, took
Paul and brought him by night to Antipatris. 32 But on
the morrow they left the horsemen to go with him, and returned to the castle: 33 and they, when they came to
Cæsarea and delivered the letter to the governor, presented
Paul also before him. 34 And when he had read it, he
asked of what province he was; and when he understood
that he was of Cilicia, 35 I will hear thee fully, said he,
when thine accusers also are come: and he commanded
him to be kept in Herod's palace.*

The first link in the chain of circumstances which
brought Paul from Jerusalem to Rome was a plot formed
against his life by the Jews. Forty of them bound themselves by a curse neither to eat nor to drink until they had
killed him. They went to the chief council of the nation
and formed a conspiracy by which the rulers were to request that Paul be brought before them for further examination, with the understanding, however, that the murderers should thus have the opportunity of accomplishing
their crime while the prisoner was being led to the court.
What is here emphasized is not only the villainy of the
assassins, but the utter degradation of the national council
and thus the hopeless apostasy of the Jewish nation.

The discovery and defeat of the foul plot were due to the
alertness of Paul's nephew. Usually there is not much
going on that escapes the knowledge of a small boy; but
how this lad knew the plans of these murderers it is difficult to conjecture. Nor can one tell how he secured access
to his uncle as the bearer of the dark secret. Paul, however, sent the boy to the chief captain who at once realized
the seriousness of the situation and the peril of his mysterious prisoner. He saw that the life of a Roman citizen
was threatened by the Jews of Jerusalem. No precautions
were neglected. An escort was prepared of foot soldiers
and cavalry forming a strong military guard, and Paul was

sent by night to Antipatris and thence to Caesarea, where he would be under the care of the Roman governor Felix. The minute details are picturesque and full of interest and also emphasize the point of the narrative which is to show how much more secure life and justice were in the hands of a heathen government than under the degenerate rulers of the professed people of God.

The "chief captain," Claudius Lysias, sent with Paul a letter, addressed to Felix, in which as far as possible he set forth the facts in the case. The letter (ch. 23:26-30) opens with a palpable lie; the officer affirms that he rescued Paul from the mob when he learned that he was a Roman; in reality when he arrested Paul he supposed him to be an Egyptian rebel. The intimation is that Roman law secured justice even when its officials were far from trustworthy. Nevertheless the general impression made upon the reader by the sketch of this old Roman is, in the main, favorable. He knows his duty, he is prompt in action, he is loyal to the Empire and proud of its citizenship, he is courteous to Paul and even gentle to his nephew; in this letter he does all he can for the welfare of the apostle, stating that he has "nothing laid to his charge worthy of death or of bonds." Even this sturdy soldier forms a striking contrast to the Jewish high priest. Every item of the narrative emphasizes the depth to which the Jewish nation has fallen and the comparative honor of the Roman government.

The first governor before whom Paul appeared was, however, a man of ignoble character. He learned the province to which Paul belonged and then remanded him to prison until his accusers should arrive from Jerusalem.

5. PAUL BEFORE FELIX   Ch. 24

1 And after five days the high priest Ananias came down with certain elders, and with an orator, one Tertullus; and they informed the governor against Paul. 2 And when he was called, Tertullus began to accuse him, saying,

Seeing that by thee we enjoy much peace, and that by thy providence evils are corrected for this nation, 3 we accept it in all ways and in all places, most excellent Felix, with all thankfulness. 4 But, that I be not further tedious unto thee, I entreat thee to hear us of thy clemency a few words. 5 For we have found this man a pestilent fellow, and a mover of insurrections among all the Jews throughout the world, and a ringleader of the sect of the Nazarenes: 6 who moreover assayed to profane the temple: on whom also we laid hold: 8 from whom thou wilt be able, by examining him thyself, to take knowledge of all these things whereof we accuse him. 9 And the Jews also joined in the charge, affirming that these things were so.

10 And when the governor had beckoned unto him to speak, Paul answered,

Forasmuch as I know that thou hast been of many years a judge unto this nation, I cheerfully make my defence: 11 seeing that thou canst take knowledge that it is not more than twelve days since I went up to worship at Jerusalem: 12 and neither in the temple did they find me disputing with any man or stirring up a crowd, nor in the synagogues, nor in the city. 13 Neither can they prove to thee the things whereof they now accuse me. 14 But this I confess unto thee, that after the Way which they call a sect, so serve I the God of our fathers, believing all things which are according to the law, and which are written in the prophets; 15 having hope toward God, which these also themselves look for, that there shall be a resurrection both of the just and unjust. 16 Herein I also exercise myself to have a conscience void of offence toward God and men always. 17 Now after some years I came to bring alms to my nation, and offerings: 18 amidst which they found me purified in the temple, with no crowd, nor yet with tumult: but there were certain Jews from Asia—19 who ought to have been here before thee, and to make accusation, if they had aught against me. 20 Or else let these men themselves say what wrong-doing they found when I stood before the council, 21 except it be for this one voice, that I cried standing among them, Touching the resurrection of the dead I am called in question before you this day.

22 But Felix, having more exact knowledge concerning

the Way, deferred them, saying, When Lysias the chief cap-
tain shall come down, I will determine your matter.   23
And he gave order to the centurion that he should be kept
in charge, and should have indulgence; and not to forbid
any of his friends to minister unto him.

24 But after certain days, Felix came with Drusilla, his
wife, who was a Jewess, and sent for Paul, and heard him
concerning the faith in Christ Jesus.   25 And as he rea-
soned of righteousness, and self-control, and the judgment
to come, Felix was terrified, and answered, Go thy way for
this time; and when I have a convenient season, I will call
thee unto me.   26 He hoped withal that money would be
given him of Paul: wherefore also he sent for him the
oftener, and communed with him.   27 But when two years
were fulfilled, Felix was succeeded by Porcius Festus; and
desiring to gain favor with the Jews, Felix left Paul in
bonds.

The cause of Paul was prejudiced and his life was imperiled by his being placed on trial before a judge of such
cruel and profligate character as Felix.   However, the historian gives no description of this Roman governor, and
allows his character to reveal itself only in part, and that
as the chapter draws to a close.   The design of the writer
is to reveal the innocence of Paul, and thus the increasing
and shameless ignominy of his enemies, the Jews.   The
latter are represented by the high priest and other rulers,
and they bring with them as their spokesman an orator
named Tertullus.   The endeavor of the Jews is to prove
Paul a criminal and thus to show themselves innocent in
rejecting the gospel he preaches.   How eagerly men seek
an excuse for rejecting Christ; and yet by such rejection
one is already self-condemned!

The speech of Tertullus opens with such empty bombast
as to be really ludicrous.   He praises the "most excellent
Felix" for the quiet and order his government has secured,
knowing perfectly well that greater abuses had never been
allowed to exist, and that if the governor had suppressed
a few bandits, it was only because he coveted their booty

for himself. The orator then designates Paul as a man of
evil character, and brings three definite indictments against
him: first, he declares him guilty of sedition, then of
heresy, and lastly of sacrilege.

When the Jewish witnesses have perjured themselves in
swearing to the truth of these false charges, Paul defends
himself by arguments which are clear and convincing. He
pays the only possible compliment which an honest man
could offer to Felix, namely, that the governor has had
ample opportunity to become acquainted with Jewish law
and customs; it is a shrewd intimation that the charges concern such matters and involve no real crime. Paul dis-
dains to notice the aspersion on his character made by
Tertullus, but answers his three charges in the order in
which they have been made. As to sedition, it is absurd
to suppose Paul guilty, for he had been in Jerusalem less
than a week; even in that short time he had addressed no
assembly and had gathered no crowd; there is further not
a shred of evidence to support the charge.

As to heresy, he frankly confesses that he is a Christian,
but as such he accepts the whole of the Old Testament, the
Scriptures held sacred by the Jews, he holds the glorious
hope therein set forth, and in its power has kept his conscience void of offense.

As to the last charge, he shows that instead of treating
the Jewish Holy Place as profane, he had come to Jerusalem to bring alms to the people and offerings to the
Temple, where he was engaged in performing the most
sacred rites when he was falsely accused and arrested;
moreover, those who so accused him are not now present,
and the Jews who are accusing him are not competent
witnesses; the latter have already investigated his case in
their own chief tribunal and have found that his only fault
is his professed belief in a doctrine of "resurrection" which
many of the members of that tribunal themselves believe.

The argument was unanswerable; even Felix could not
question its force; but wishing to please the Jews he pre-

tended to withhold his decision until the arrival of Lysias from Jerusalem. In fact, however, he already had the favorable testimony of this "chief captain"; and in giving Paul the largest possible liberty he virtually acquitted the apostle.

When Paul was given a further hearing before Felix and his sinful wife, Paul reasoned with such power as to "righteousness, and self-control, and the judgment to come," that the guilty Felix was terrified, and declared that he would hear Paul further at a more convenient time. This, of course, was a mere flimsy excuse for not reforming his own life and for denying justice to Paul. The real cause of delay and indecision was his enslavement to sin and his hope that delay would result in the offer of a bribe by the friends of the apostle. The result was that Paul was kept a prisoner for two years, until Felix was succeeded as governor by Porcius Festus.

6. PAUL'S APPEAL TO CAESAR   Ch. 25

1 Festus therefore, having come into the province, after three days went up to Jerusalem from Cæsarea. 2 And the chief priests and the principal men of the Jews informed him against Paul; and they besought him, 3 asking a favor against him, that he would send for him to Jerusalem; laying a plot to kill him on the way. 4 Howbeit Festus answered, that Paul was kept in charge at Cæsarea, and that he himself was about to depart thither shortly. 5 Let them therefore, saith he, that are of power among you go down with me, and if there is anything amiss in the man, let them accuse him.

6 And when he had tarried among them not more than eight or ten days, he went down unto Cæsarea; and on the morrow he sat on the judgment-seat, and commanded Paul to be brought. 7 And when he was come, the Jews that had come down from Jerusalem stood round about him, bringing against him many and grievous charges which they could not prove; 8 while Paul said in his defence, Neither against the law of the Jews, nor against the temple, nor against Cæsar, have I sinned at all.   9 But Festus, desiring to gain favor with the Jews, answered Paul and said, Wilt thou go up to Jerusalem, and there be judged of these things before me?   10 But Paul said, I am standing before Cæsar's judgment-seat, where I ought to be judged: to the Jews have I done no wrong, as thou also very well knowest.   11 If then I am a wrong-doer, and have committed anything worthy of death, I refuse not to die; but if none of those things is true whereof these accuse me, no man can give me up unto them.   I appeal unto Cæsar.   12 Then Festus, when he had conferred with the council, answered, Thou hast appealed unto Cæsar: unto Cæsar shalt thou go.

13 Now when certain days were passed, Agrippa the king and Bernice arrived at Cæsarea, and saluted Festus. 14 And as they tarried there many days, Festus laid Paul's case before the king, saying, There is a certain man left a prisoner by Felix;   15 about whom, when I was at Jerusalem, the chief priests and the elders of the Jews informed me, asking for sentence against him.   16 To whom I answered, that it is not the custom of the Romans to give up any man, before that the accused have the accusers face to face, and have had opportunity to make his defence concerning the matter laid against him.   17 When therefore they were come together here, I made no delay, but on the next day sat on the judgment-seat, and commanded the man to be brought.   18 Concerning whom, when the accusers stood up, they brought no charge of such evil things as I supposed;   19 but had certain questions against him of their own religion, and of one Jesus, who was dead, whom Paul affirmed to be alive.   20 And I, being perplexed how to inquire concerning these things, asked whether he would go to Jerusalem and there be judged of these matters.   21 But when Paul had appealed to be kept for the decision of the emperor, I commanded him to be kept till I should send him to Cæsar.   22 And Agrippa said unto Festus, I also could wish to hear the man myself.   To-morrow, saith he, thou shalt hear him.

23 So on the morrow, when Agrippa was come, and Bernice, with great pomp, and they were entered into the place of hearing with the chief captains and the principal men of the city, at the command of Festus Paul was brought in. 24 And Festus saith, King Agrippa, and all men who are here present with us, ye behold this man, about whom all the multitude of the Jews made suit to me, both at Jerusalem and here, crying that he ought not to live any longer. 25 But I found that he had committed nothing worthy of death: and as he himself appealed to the emperor I determined to send him. 26 Of whom I have no certain thing to write unto my lord. Wherefore I have brought him forth before you, and specially before thee, king Agrippa, that, after examination had, I may have somewhat to write. 27 For it seemeth to me unreasonable, in sending a prisoner, not withal to signify the charges against him.

Paul's appeal to Caesar was due to no impatience or anger or cowardice on his part, but rather to the indecision, injustice, and treachery of a Roman ruler. Porcius Festus was a man of higher character than Felix, whom he succeeded as governor, but his discreditable conduct toward Paul brings into clear relief the innocence of the apostle and thus further emphasizes the guilt of the Jews, who were falsely accusing him and were seeking his life. In fact, the whole burden of these closing chapters of The Acts is the sin of Israel in rejecting the gospel as it is represented in the preaching and the person of the apostle.

Festus was a man of restless activity, and true to his nature, only three days after his appointment he paid a visit to Jerusalem. Two years had passed since Paul was rescued from the Jewish mob, and carried prisoner to Caesarea; but the Jews were still the same, both in their hatred of Paul and in their utter moral abasement. They reported to the Roman governor that Paul was a vile criminal who "ought not to live any longer" and they requested that he be brought to Jerusalem for trial "laying a plot to kill him on the way." We take it for granted that the forty assassins, who many months before "bound themselves under a curse, saying that they would neither eat nor drink till they had killed Paul," had meanwhile allowed them-

selves some refreshment; but their spirit or that of their
successors was unchanged, and it must be remembered that
these murderers represented the chief council, and therefore the nation, of the Jews. Festus properly refused the
request and advised the Jewish rulers to come to Caesarea
in case they wished to bring charges against Paul. A few
days later, followed closely by the Jewish rulers, he returned to Caesarea and immediately summoned Paul before his judgment seat. Of this trial no details are given;
the story is becoming too monotonous; the innocence of
Paul has been established repeatedly. As usual the Jews
again brought "against him many and grievous charges
which they could not prove"; it is perfectly evident that
the Jews had no case against the apostle but were mad
with hatred because of his bold and unwavering allegiance
to Christ.

Festus, however, desired to gain favor with the Jews,
and therefore asked Paul whether he was willing to go to
Jerusalem for trial; but why for trial, when the innocence
of Paul was already clear to the judge; and why to Jerusalem, where the life of Paul would be imperiled by Jewish
assassins? If death were deserved or could accomplish
good, Paul was ready to die, but if it was merely to gratify
thirst for blood, and if the Roman governor was unwilling
to defend an innocent Roman citizen, there was but one
thing to do, namely, to appeal to the decision of the emperor.

To the cry of Paul, "I appeal unto Cæsar," there was
but one reply that Festus could properly make: "Unto
Cæsar shalt thou go"; but the decision placed Festus in a
most awkward predicament. He had now to send to
Rome an innocent man against whom he was unable to
formulate any charges which would stand in a Roman
court. How then would Festus himself appear as an ad-
ministrator of justice in a Roman province when at last
all the facts should be presented to the emperor? The
situation was painfully embarrassing, yet into just such

places do men bring themselves when they seek to win favor by acting contrary to conscience, and when they reverse decisions which they know to be right.

Nevertheless, God overruled the fault of Festus and by it effected his purpose to bring Paul to Rome. Even before the apostle sailed, the distress of Festus afforded Paul an opportunity of preaching the gospel before the most distinguished and powerful audience he had ever faced.

The occasion was a visit paid to Festus by King Agrippa, the son of that Herod who had beheaded James and imprisoned Peter. The Roman governor thought that Agrippa, a Jew, might be able to find in the prisoner, whom the Jews so hated, some wrong which Festus could frame as a charge when Paul should be sent to Rome. He therefore rehearsed the story to the king, but was careful to conceal his own injustice and treachery in the case. Two things he made clear, however: first, that Paul was innocent of any crime; second, that the essential point in the gospel which Paul preached and the main cause of Jewish hatred lay in the doctrine of the resurrection.

To the delight of Festus his royal guest was eager to hear Paul speak. No time was lost, and on the next day a brilliant company assembled to listen to Paul's greatest and last recorded defense. Here Paul enjoyed certain great advantages. His judges already believed him guiltless of serious fault; none of his Jewish enemies were present to present their false charges; he could speak with freedom and could state fully the facts of his conversion from Judaism and of his relation to Christ. Thus, while the address is intensely personal, it is of immense value as a defense of Christianity, as a statement of its relation to Judaism, and as an exhibition of its character as a religion for the whole world.

7. PAUL'S DEFENSE BEFORE KING AGRIPPA
Ch. 26

*1 And Agrippa said unto Paul, Thou art permitted to
speak for thyself. Then Paul stretched forth his hand, and
made his defence:*

*2 I think myself happy, king Agrippa, that I am to make
my defence before thee this day touching all the things
whereof I am accused by the Jews: 3 especially because
thou are expert in all customs and questions which are
among the Jews: wherefore I beseech thee to hear me pa-
tiently. 4 My manner of life then from my youth up,
which was from the beginning among mine own nation and
at Jerusalem, know all the Jews; 5 having knowledge of
me from the first, if they be willing to testify, that after
the straitest sect of our religion I lived a Pharisee. 6 And
now I stand here to be judged for the hope of the promise
made of God unto our fathers; 7 unto which promise our
twelve tribes, earnestly serving God night and day, hope
to attain. And concerning this hope I am accused by the
Jews, O king! 8 Why is it judged incredible with you, if
God doth raise the dead? 9 I verily thought with myself
that I ought to do many things contrary to the name of
Jesus of Nazareth. 10 And this I also did in Jerusalem:
and I both shut up many of the saints in prisons, having
received authority from the chief priests, and when they
were put to death I gave my vote against them. 11 And
punishing them oftentimes in all the synagogues, I strove
to make them blaspheme; and being exceedingly mad
against them, I persecuted them even unto foreign cities.
12 Whereupon as I journeyed to Damascus with the authority and commission of the chief priests, 13 at midday,
O king, I saw on the way a light from heaven, above the
brightness of the sun, shining round about me and them
that journeyed with me. 14 And when we were all fallen
to the earth, I heard a voice saying unto me in the Hebrew
language, Saul, Saul, why persecutest thou me? it is hard
for thee to kick against the goad. 15 And I said, Who art
thou, Lord? And the Lord said, I am Jesus whom thou
persecutest. 16 But arise, and stand upon thy feet: for*

to this end have I appeared unto thee, to appoint thee a minister and a witness both of the things wherein thou hast seen me, and of the things wherein I will appear unto thee; 17 delivering thee from the people, and from the Gentiles, unto whom I send thee, 18 to open their eyes, that they may turn from darkness to light and from the power of Satan unto God, that they may receive remission of sins and an inheritance among them that are sanctified by faith in me. 19 Wherefore, O king Agrippa, I was not disobedient unto the heavenly vision: 20 but declared both to them of Damascus first, and at Jerusalem, and throughout all the country of Judæa, and also to the Gentiles, that they should repent and turn to God, doing works worthy of repentance. 21 For this cause the Jews seized me in the temple, and assayed to kill me. 22 Having therefore obtained the help that is from God, I stand unto this day testifying both to small and great, saying nothing but what the prophets and Moses did say should come; 23 how that the Christ must suffer, and how that he first by the resurrection of the dead should proclaim light both to the people and to the Gentiles.

24 And as he thus made his defence, Festus saith with a loud voice, Paul, thou art mad; thy much learning is turning thee mad. 25 But Paul saith, I am not mad, most excellent Festus; but speak forth words of truth and soberness. 26 For the king knoweth of these things, unto whom also I speak freely: for I am persuaded that none of these things is hidden from him; for this hath not been done in a corner. 27 King Agrippa, believest thou the prophets? I know that thou believest. 28 And Agrippa said unto Paul, With but little persuasion thou wouldest fain make me a Christian. 29 And Paul said, I would to God, that whether with little or with much, not thou only, but also all that hear me this day, might become such as I am, except these bonds.

30 And the king rose up, and the governor, and Bernice, and they that sat with them: 31 and when they had withdrawn, they spake one to another, saying, This man doeth nothing worthy of death or of bonds. 32 And Agrippa said unto Festus, This man might have been set at liberty, if he had not appealed unto Cæsar.

Paul's address before Agrippa is much more than a defense of his own innocence or a review of his personal religious experience; it is a superb statement of the very essence of Christianity, and as one reads this historic speech two or three of its propositions should be especially noted. Paul insists that faith in a risen, divine Christ is the very heart of Christianity, that the resurrection is attested by competent human witnesses and by inspired Scriptures, and that the message of salvation through Christ is intended for the whole race of mankind.

The introductory sentences are conciliatory. Paul pays to King Agrippa about the only compliment which would have been honest. Agrippa was "expert in all customs and questions . . . among the Jews," and as Paul has been accused by Jews in matters exclusively Jewish and religious, he is "happy" to present his case before such a judge. At once, however, Paul is implying that inasmuch as the matters are thus Jewish and religious, he is innocent of any crime which Roman law will recognize.

As to the actual charge of heresy or sacrilege, for which he appears as a prisoner, Paul at once shows that it is absurd, for he is himself a Jew of the strictest sect, and he is held guilty because he believes and teaches the essential doctrine of Judaism, namely, the hope of a Messiah. He is thus innocent in the view of Roman law, for Judaism is a religion permitted by Rome; quite as evidently he cannot be accused as a heretic by the Jews.

However, there are two points in reference to the Messiah in which Paul does differ from his fellow Jews: one is his belief that Jesus of Nazareth is the promised Messiah, and the other is his message that, through faith in Jesus, Gentiles as well as Jews can be saved. The resurrection of Jesus has convinced Paul that he is the Christ. To Jews the fact of resurrection is not a thing "judged incredible," and the fact that Jesus has risen, is a truth in favor of which Paul has not been prejudiced; indeed he once fiercely persecuted all who so believed; but on his

way to Damascus he actually saw Jesus, risen and glorified, and thus he cannot longer question his claims or
doubt his saving power. As to his preaching to the Gentiles, Paul shows that this was not a self-imposed task but
in obedience to a commission received personally from his
divine Lord. It was couched in words which each follower
of Christ does well to keep in mind as he today looks out
upon a world in darkness and misery and sin: "I send
thee, to open their eyes, that they may turn from darkness
to light and from the power of Satan unto God, that they
may receive remission of sins and an inheritance among
them that are sanctified by faith in me."

How, then, could Paul be "disobedient unto the heavenly vision," how could he fail to preach repentance and
faith in Christ "at Jerusalem, and throughout all the country of Judæa, and also to the Gentiles," and how could the
Jews be justified in having "seized" him in the Temple and
"assayed to kill" him? After all, the Jews, and not he,
should be charged with heresy, for the Old Testament
Scriptures had testified that the Christ was to suffer and
to rise again, and was to be the Source of light and life,
both to Jews and to Gentiles; truly, therefore, one could
be guilty of no fault if he accepted Jesus as the Messiah
and testified for him "to small and great."

As this defense was being delivered by Paul, the pagan
Festus heard little that he could understand, and as Paul
spoke of the resurrection of a crucified Jew, and of light
and life being brought into the world through him, he
became impatient and cried out in ignorant intolerance,
"Paul, thou art mad." To this Paul replied with compo-
sure and courtesy, and then turned earnestly to Agrippa.
The king must have understood all that Paul had been
saying. To him the arguments could not have been without force, particularly those based on the Old Testament.
"King Agrippa," cried the apostle, "believest thou the
prophets? I know that thou believest." But the king
would not allow himself so easily to be summoned as a

witness in behalf of the despised Nazarenes. With disdainful irony he replied, "With but little persuasion thou wouldest fain make me a Christian." Then Paul, with a spiritual vision which saw human life in true perspective, and as one who appreciated through faith in Christ such joys as kings and princes might well envy, cried, with the fervor of a seer, "I would to God, that whether with little or with much, not thou only, but also all that hear me this day, might become such as I am, except these bonds."

Thus closes the last great defense of the apostle. The judges rendered their decision: Paul was innocent; but what shall be said of Festus, whose injustice has compelled Paul to appeal to Caesar, or what of the Jews, who in delivering Paul to the Romans have finally rejected their Messiah, his Master and Lord?

F. PAUL'S JOURNEY TO ROME Chs. 27; 28

1. THE VOYAGE AND SHIPWRECK   Ch. 27

1 And when it was determined that we should sail for Italy, they delivered Paul and certain other prisoners to a centurion named Julius, of the Augustan band. 2 And embarking in a ship of Adramyttium, which was about to sail unto the places on the coast of Asia, we put to sea, Aristarchus, a Macedonian of Thessalonica, being with us. 3 And the next day we touched at Sidon: and Julius treated Paul kindly, and gave him leave to go unto his friends and refresh himself. 4 And putting to sea from thence, we sailed under the lee of Cyprus, because the winds were contrary. 5 And when we had sailed across the sea which is off Cilicia and Pamphylia, we came to Myra, a city of Lycia. 6 And there the centurion found a ship of Alexandria sailing for Italy; and he put us therein. 7 And when we had sailed slowly many days, and were come with difficulty over against Cnidus, the wind not further suffering us, we sailed under the lee of Crete, over against Salmone; 8 and with difficulty coasting along it we came unto a certain place called Fair Havens; nigh whereunto was the city of Lasea.

9 And when much time was spent, and the voyage was now dangerous, because the Fast was now already gone by, Paul admonished them, 10 and said unto them, Sirs, I perceive that the voyage will be with injury and much loss, not only of the lading and the ship, but also of our lives. 11 But the centurion gave more heed to the master and to the owner of the ship, than to those things which were spoken by Paul. 12 And because the haven was not commodious to winter in, the more part advised to put to sea from thence, if by any means they could reach Phœnix, and winter there; which is a haven of Crete, looking north-east and south-east. 13 And when the south wind blew softly, supposing that they had obtained their purpose, they weighed anchor and sailed along Crete, close in shore. 14 But after no long time there beat down from it a tempestuous wind, which is called Euraquilo: 15 and when the ship was caught, and could not face the wind, we gave way to it, and were driven. 16 And running under the lee of a small island called Cauda, we were able, with difficulty, to secure the boat: 17 and when they had hoisted it up, they used helps, under-girding the ship; and, fearing lest they should be cast upon the Syrtis, they lowered the gear, and so were driven. 18 And as we labored exceedingly with the storm, the next day they began to throw the freight *overboard; 19 and the third day they cast out with their own hands the tackling of the ship. 20 And when neither sun nor stars shone upon us for many days, and no small tempest lay on us, all hope that we should be saved was now taken away. 21 And when they had been long without food, then Paul stood forth in the midst of them, and said, Sirs, ye should have hearkened unto me, and not have set sail from Crete, and have gotten this injury and loss. 22 And now I exhort you to be of good cheer; for there shall be no loss of life among you, but only of the ship. 23 For there stood by me this night an angel of the God whose I am, whom also I serve, 24 saying, Fear not, Paul; thou must stand before Cæsar: and lo, God hath granted thee all them that sail with thee. 25 Wherefore, sirs, be of good cheer: for I believe God, that it shall be even so as it hath been spoken unto me. 26 But we must be cast upon a certain island.*

27 But when the fourteenth night was come, as we were driven to and fro in the sea of Adria, about midnight the sailors surmised that they were drawing near to some country: 28 and they sounded, and found twenty fathoms; and after a little space, they sounded again, and found fifteen fathoms. 29 And fearing lest haply we should be cast ashore on rocky ground, they let go four anchors from the stern, and wished for the day. 30 And as the sailors were seeking to flee out of the ship, and had lowered the boat into the sea, under color as though they would lay out anchors from the foreship, 31 Paul said to the centurion and to the soldiers, Except these abide in the ship, ye cannot be saved. 32 Then the soldiers cut away the ropes of the boat, and let her fall off. 33 And while the day was coming on, Paul besought them all to take some food, saying, This day is the fourteenth day that ye wait and continue fasting, having taken nothing. 34 Wherefore I beseech you to take some food: for this is for your safety: for there shall not a hair perish from the head of any of you. 35 And when he had said this, and had taken bread, he gave thanks to God in the presence of all; and he brake it, and began to eat. 36 Then were they all of good cheer, and themselves also took food. 37 And we were in all in the ship two hundred threescore and sixteen souls. 38 And when they had eaten enough, they lightened the ship, throwing out the wheat into the sea. 39 And when it was day, they knew not the land: but they perceived a certain bay with a beach, and they took counsel whether they could drive the ship upon it. 40 And casting off the anchors, they left them in the sea, at the same time loosing the bands of the rudders; and hoisting up the foresail to the wind, they made for the beach. 41 But lighting upon a place where two seas met, they ran the vessel aground; and the foreship struck and remained unmoveable, but the stern began to break up by the violence of the waves. 42 And the soldiers' counsel was to kill the prisoners, lest any of them should swim out, and escape. 43 But the centurion, desiring to save Paul, stayed them from their purpose; and commanded that they who could swim should cast themselves overboard, and get first to the land; 44 and the rest, some on planks, and some on other things from the ship.

And so it came to pass, that they all escaped safe to the land.

No story of the sea is more fascinating, none is more widely known, than the record of the shipwreck suffered by Paul and his companions on their journey to Rome. One of these companions was Luke, the author of The Acts, and it is easy to understand why he writes with such graphic minuteness of detail; he is describing the most thrilling and perilous adventure of his life, and further he is depicting scenes in which the central figure is that of his great hero, Paul. However, Luke is a historian of the first rank; in every other section of his narrative he has shown a careful selection of material, a subordination of detail, a continual emphasis upon the main purpose of his treatise; is he here allowing personal experiences or the admiration of a friend to mar the symmetry of his work, and this at its very climax? Of course, this shipwreck was a part of the history he is writing, but there must have been something more than the dramatic character of the event to make Luke feel that he should describe it at such length. What, then, has been his purpose in these closing chapters of The Acts? Has it not been to show how the gospel was rejected by the Jews, and how the future center of its proclamation was not to be Jerusalem but Rome? How, then, could these facts be impressed on the reader more artistically than by an absorbing story told at great length and separating the experiences of the apostle in the province of Judea from those which were his in the capital city of the Empire?

Whatever the special purpose of the author, the story contains a new revelation of the striking personality of Paul, and prepares the reader for his great Epistles which follow. Then, too, there appear on the very surface of the narrative lessons of practical importance both for Christian life and service.

The story pictures Paul's being sent to Rome as a prisoner. There is much to lessen the distress of this cruel experience: He goes as an innocent man in whom the governor who sends him can find no fault; Rome long has been the goal of his ambition; he has been assured that the journey is in fulfillment of a divine purpose; he is allowed the help of two comrades, one of them a "beloved physician"; he enjoys the confidence, even the affection, of the Roman officer who has in charge the company of prisoners with whom he is to travel. This soldier, like Cornelius, and like the two other centurions described in the New Testament, seems to have been a man of high character, who was at once attracted by the personality of Paul and who finally endangers his life to save the life of the apostle. The very first day after putting to sea the vessel touches at Sidon, and there Luke says, the centurion "treated Paul kindly, and gave him leave to go unto his friends and refresh himself."

Following the usual trade route northward and westward they reach Myra on the coast of Lycia, and there change vessels, embarking on a ship from Alexandria which is bound for Italy. They sail to the island of Crete and stop at a place called Fair Havens, where Paul advises them to winter; his advice however is overruled and a harbor is sought farther west. Hardly has the ill-fated ship put to sea, when she is caught by a fierce gale; with difficulty the lifeboat is drawn aboard, the ship is strengthened by cables, and then allowed to drive before the wind. The following day the storm increases and it seems necessary to cast overboard the freight and all unnecessary tackle. Then for fourteen days and nights, with all bearings lost, without sight of sun or stars, the voyagers are at the mercy of the tempest until all hope is abandoned. Then Paul appears as the great heroic figure whose dauntless courage gives new heart to his companions; he rebukes them for disregarding his advice, but assures them that the God he serves has sent a message declaring that they are all to be saved but that they will be wrecked on a certain island.

For intelligent men, however, the assurance of a divine purpose and promise never lessens the need for human action and effort. Paul is alert, and practically assumes command of the ship. As in the night the soundings show that they are being driven toward a strange coast, and as the sailors try to escape with the boat, Paul declares that the sailors must remain on board or all will be lost. Anchors have been thrown from the stern of the ship and all on board are longing for day. Again Paul speaks words of hope and urges all to break their long fast; he sets the example, but first, before them all, he returns thanks to God for the food and then encourages them to eat. The refreshment is needed, for at daybreak as they seek to thrust the ship into a sheltering bay, she is caught by the waves, driven upon the beach, and soon broken in pieces; but, as Paul promised, by swimming, or by clinging to broken pieces of the wreck, every one of the ship's company is rescued.

How often followers of Christ have had the experience of Paul, and in time of storm and peril have been assured of the presence and power and protection of their Lord; how often, too, has their faith made them appear heroic figures towering above all their comrades both in courage and in promptness of action, as they have testified by word and deed to the goodness of their Lord! How often, too, when the cause of Christ has been imperiled, has it been found that through all storms and tempests a divine hand is still in control, and that there is being achieved the divine purpose of bringing the gospel into all the world and to every creature.

2. THE STAY AT MELITA   Ch. 28:1-10

1 And when we were escaped, then we knew that the island was called Melita. 2 And the barbarians showed us no common kindness: for they kindled a fire, and received us all, because of the present rain, and because of the cold. 3 But when Paul had gathered a bundle of sticks and laid them on the fire, a viper came out by reason of the heat, and fastened on his hand. 4 And when the barbarians saw the venomous creature hanging from his hand, they said one to another, No doubt this man is a murderer, whom, though he hath escaped from the sea, yet Justice hath not suffered to live. 5 Howbeit he shook off the creature into the fire, and took no harm. 6 But they expected that he would have swollen, or fallen down dead suddenly: but when they were long in expectation and beheld nothing amiss come to him, they changed their minds, and said that he was a god.

7 Now in the neighborhood of that place were lands belonging to the chief man of the island, named Publius; who received us, and entertained us three days courteously. 8 And it was so, that the father of Publius lay sick of fever and dysentery: unto whom Paul entered in, and prayed, and laying his hands on him healed him. 9 And when this was done, the rest also that had diseases in the island came, and were cured: 10 who also honored us with many honors; and when we sailed, they put on board such things as we needed.

The Jewish chief priests and the Roman governors in Judea form a pitiful contrast to the "barbarians" of Melita and "the chief man of the island." The former were plotting against Paul's life and imprisoning him as a felon; the latter showed him "no common kindness" and came to regard him as a god. The hospitality shown by these islanders to the shipwrecked company forms a very beautiful picture. On the winter morning, in a chilling rain, running to the beach, they drag from the breakers the weary, terrified survivors of the wreck; they build for them a fire and seek to do all in their power to relieve discomfort and distress. The gospel, rejected by the Jews, is being carried to the heathen; and these natives of Melita are not the last to show that human sympathy is universal, or the last to offer kindness to the missionary of the cross.

An incident now occurs which deeply impresses "the barbarians." Paul is of course helping with the fire; he is throwing on a bundle of sticks which he has gathered, when suddenly a viper, driven from the fire by the heat, fastens itself on his hand. The natives know well that the bite is deadly; they at once conclude that Paul must be a murderer, who, escaping from the sea, is now overtaken by divine justice. Surely the heathen have consciences which accuse them and which teach them that wrong will be punished and that the soul that sins must die; what they lack is not so much the sense of sin, as the knowledge of how they can be saved. But when these natives see that Paul suffers no harm from the poisonous bite, which they have supposed fatal, they change their minds and say that he is "a god."

This experience must have been of secret comfort to the apostle; he must have recalled the promise of Christ that when his messengers should begin their work of preaching the gospel to every creature he would be with them, and, among other "signs," they should "take up serpents" and be unharmed. For some men the bite of a viper, as truly as the visit of an angel, is an occasion for rejoicing in the presence and protection of the Lord.

Such an extraordinary visitor as Paul is speedily brought to the home of "the chief man of the island, named Publius" and there with his friends he is courteously entertained for three days. The father of Publius is seriously ill, but as Paul prays he is instantly healed; the news spreads among the natives and we are told that "the rest also that had diseases in the island came, and were cured."

The church no longer needs to depend upon miracles, but bodily healing at the hands of missionaries is still effective in opening the way for the gospel message. That Paul proclaimed the gospel to these men of Melita there can be no doubt; Luke, however, makes no mention of the fact, he only intimates that as Paul had been the chief instrument in saving the lives of the great company on the wrecked ship, so it was due to the favor he won from the natives that this same company was hospitably entertained for three months and finally left the island "honored . . . with many honors," and with such things as they needed for their remaining journey to Rome.

3. PAUL'S RECEPTION IN ROME   Ch. 28:11-31

11 And after three months we set sail in a ship of Alexandria which had wintered in the island, whose sign was The Twin Brothers. 12 And touching at Syracuse, we tarried there three days. 13 And from thence we made a circuit, and arrived at Rhegium: and after one day a south wind sprang up, and on the second day we came to Puteoli; 14 where we found brethren, and were entreated to tarry with them seven days: and so we came to Rome. 15 And from thence the brethren, when they heard of us, came to meet us as far as The Market of Appius and The Three Taverns; whom when Paul saw, he thanked God, and took courage.

16 And when we entered into Rome, Paul was suffered to abide by himself with the soldier that guarded him.

17 And it came to pass, that after three days he called together those that were the chief of the Jews: and when they were come together, he said unto them, I, brethren, though I had done nothing against the people, or the customs of our fathers, yet was delivered prisoner from Jerusalem into the hands of the Romans: 18 who, when they had examined me, desired to set me at liberty, because there was no cause of death in me. 19 But when the Jews spake against it, I was constrained to appeal unto Cæsar; not that I had aught whereof to accuse my nation. 20 For this cause therefore did I entreat you to see and to speak with me: for because of the hope of Israel I am bound with this chain. 21 And they said unto him, We neither received letters from Judæa concerning thee, nor did any of the brethren come hither and report or speak any harm of thee. 22 But we desire to hear of thee what thou thinkest: for as concerning this sect, it is known to us that everywhere it is spoken against.

23 And when they had appointed him a day, they came to him into his lodging in great number; to whom he ex-

pounded the matter, *testifying the kingdom of God, and persuading them concerning Jesus, both from the law of Moses and from the prophets, from morning till evening. 24 And some believed the things which were spoken, and some disbelieved. 25 And when they agreed not among themselves, they departed after that Paul had spoken one word, Well spake the Holy Spirit through Isaiah the prophet unto your fathers, 26 saying,*

> *Go thou unto this people, and say,*
> *By hearing ye shall hear, and shall in no wise understand;*
> *And seeing ye shall see, and shall in no wise perceive:*
> *27 For this people's heart is waxed gross,*
> *And their ears are dull of hearing,*
> *And their eyes they have closed;*
> *Lest haply they should perceive with their eyes,*
> *And hear with their ears,*
> *And understand with their heart,*
> *And should turn again,*
> *And I should heal them.*

28 Be it known therefore unto you, that this salvation of God is sent unto the Gentiles: they will also hear.

30 And he abode two whole years in his own hired dwelling, and received all that went in unto him, 31 preaching the kingdom of God, and teaching the things concerning the Lord Jesus Christ with all boldness, none forbidding him.

The last stage of the journey to Rome is briefly narrated; the historian is now concerned with the reception given to Paul in the Imperial City, first by the church, secondly by the Roman officials, and thirdly by the Jews.

After a prosperous voyage northward from Melita, touching at Syracuse and Rhegium, Paul and his party landed at Puteoli, some one hundred and fifty miles from Rome; the cordial greeting of the Christians whom they found there made them feel that their journey was already ended. The news of Paul's arrival was carried to the city, and as he approached he found delegations from the church coming out to meet him, first at the Market of

Appius, and then at the Three Taverns, distant respectively forty-three and thirty-three miles from Rome. When Paul saw these brethren his heart was full of joy; "he thanked God, and took courage"; he knew now that the desire of his heart, the object of his prayers, was to be realized, and that in Rome he was to receive and to give that spiritual help of which he had written three years before in his great Epistle addressed to these same beloved brethren.

Paul's treatment by the Roman officials was all that could have been desired. The letter from Porcius Festus could have charged Paul with no crime; the report of the centurion Julius must have disposed the authorities to regard Paul with favor, and as the story closes, he is pictured as abiding by himself "in his own hired dwelling," receiving "all that went in unto him, preaching . . . and teaching . . . , none forbidding him."

The main interest of the story, however, turns upon the reception given to Paul by the Jews. Almost immediately upon his arrival a conference is held with their chief representatives. It is most satisfactory and promising. Paul tells them of the unjust treatment he has received, but assures them that he has no thought of bringing charges against his nation, for he is a loyal Jew and is held as a prisoner only because of his devotion to the hope which centers in the Messiah, which is the hope of all Israel. The Jews reply that no evil report concerning Paul has reached them, and that they are eager to hear what he has to say concerning the sect to which he belongs and which is everywhere spoken against. On an appointed day Paul speaks at great length, presenting the full gospel message, and proving from the Scriptures the truths concerning the death and resurrection and coming Kingdom of Christ. It is a time of solemn decision. Some accept, but as a mass the Jews reject the message. Then Paul announces the doom of the nation; even as in the days of Isaiah, a judicial blindness is visited upon Israel "until the fulness of the Gentiles be come in." Some Jews will be saved, but the nation is rejected. "Be it known therefore unto you," declares the apostle, "that this salvation of God is sent unto the Gentiles: they will also hear." Thus at the imperial center of the Gentile world the representative Jews are refusing the gospel as they have refused it in Jerusalem, and wherever Paul has preached. The doom of the nation is sealed; the sentence is pronounced by the apostle; the only hope is in a future national repentance and acceptance of Jesus of Nazareth as the Messiah and King.

The story of The Acts closes with apparent abruptness. What became of Paul? Was he released from imprisonment? To what further labors was he called? What was the end of his career? These questions are natural. We are to remember, however, that we have not been reading a life of the apostle. The Acts is a history, which tells us how the church of Christ was founded, how it was broadened from a Jewish sect to a universal brotherhood, and how it was enlarged by establishing radiating centers throughout the Empire, beginning in Jerusalem and extending to Rome. When the great apostle has reached the Imperial City, when surrounded by a group of devoted Christians he is seen "teaching the things concerning the Lord Jesus Christ . . . , none forbidding him," the story is properly ended; and it has been so narrated that the reader feels a true interest in the church and a deep desire to hasten the preaching of the gospel in all the world and to every creature.